Client Testimonials

"Jerry's ability to pick and analyze the right stocks and funds for our situation and his low-key approach has made our dream of retirement a reality. We could NOT have done it without you. Thanks, Jerry!"

Michael Povlick—Vice President, National Auto Parts
Gail Povlick—Retired

"We are, by nature "questioners." When it came time to seek answers we had the good fortune to meet Jerry Aloof. He not only provided us with "answers," but opened our eyes to the investment opportunities open to senior retirees. To us, he's the best!"

Bernard & Roslyn Ressner—Retired

"Always on the mark with investment advice, in planning, and a pleasure to work with. Come to think of it I didn't lose any money on Black Tuesday because of you. And I didn't lose my initial investments ever during the early 90's. The World Trade didn't affect me either. I made enough money to send my son to college and give my daughter a wedding. Now I just need money to retire on. Thanks Jerry!"

Julie Salzano—Intelligence Analyst

"Jerry Aloof has been my financial advisor and friend for many years. I would-n't trade him for a sack of gold. (Unless I get 17% interest!)"

Natalie Mesger—Retiree

"Since retiring approximately 10 years ago, my husband and I have reaped the benefits of Jerry managing our retirement funds. Not only does he review our accounts personally but, when needed, will recommend changes to our invest-ment mix due to more current economic situations. With Jerry at the helm of our portfolio, we are confident that we will continue to enjoy economic secu-rity in our retirement years."

Diane Giani—Supervisor (Retired)

"In times like this it's good to have a steady hand like yours on the wheel. You are our security blanket."

Robert Weiss—Merchandiser

"Jerald is much more than a financial advisor. I have known him for over 10 years, and he has always been a great educator. He has taught me more than any other person about how to invest."

Victor Catalano—Purchasing

"In the short time I have been acquainted with Jerry, I have found him to be honorable, trustworthy & extremely knowledgeable. I would recommend him highly."

Jordan Joseph—Retired

"Jerry's sincere ongoing concern and attention to my retirement portfolio, and to me as an individual client, allayed my initial apprehension and fear about investments, and instilled my trust in him as my financial advisor."

G. Harriett Schuster—Retired Teacher, B.A., M.A.

"More than an advisor, Jerry is a friend in which you can trust and he will go the extra step to help you. Good guy to have on your side."

Juan Tehume—Gas Controller (retired)

"I have always found Mr. Aloof to be honest forthright and trustworthy. His recommendations are well respected and rewarding. I have enjoyed doing business with him for (nearly) 20 years."

Joe Weiss—President
Joseph Weiss & Associates

"Over the years I have found Jerry to have up to date information. If one of my financial holdings were not doing well I would receive a call from Jerry advising me so; at that time he would inform me of another holding that was more profitable. He would then switch over to the profitable account. I have always found Jerry easy to talk to and comprehend what he is saying. I put my complete faith in Jerry; I find him to be very honest."

Louise J. Werfel—Retired Interior Designer

"It is easy to make a positive statement as it pertains to our association with Jerry Aloof and David Mattos. Throughout many years of doing business with Jerry and weathering painful market fluctuations, it seems that, at the end of the day, we survive and prosper. As a businessperson dealing with various personalities, I find doing business with Jerry and David both a good investment and personally rewarding."

Morris Gliklich—President
Top Line Wholesalers, Inc.

"Jerry has been my financial advisor for over 13 years. I consider him a friend and value his expertise. I would without question recommend Jerry to anyone as I already have."

Joel Miller—Sales Rep Cablevision

"I have been a client with Jerry for the past 10 years and have been very satisfied with his handling of my portfolio."

John L. Milewski—Retired

Rolling Over

Rolling Over

Retirement Investing in Uncertain Times

The Basics of Investing, Retirement Planning and Estate Planning

By: Jerald L. Aloof, RFC
Managing Director
JL Aloof Financial Services
Registered Financial Consultant

iUniverse, Inc.
New York Lincoln Shanghai

Rolling Over
Retirement Investing in Uncertain Times

Copyright © 2005 by Jerald L. Aloof

iUniverse books may be ordered through booksellers or by contacting:

iUniverse
2021 Pine Lake Road, Suite 100
Lincoln, NE 68512
www.iuniverse.com
1-800-Authors (1-800-288-4677)

ISBN: 0-595-33544-6

Printed in the United States of America

Disclaimer

This book contains performance data. Source: Ibbotson Associates and Morningstar. Presentation of this data is not meant to imply that similar results will be achieved in the future. Rather, past performance is no indication of future results and any assertion to the contrary is a federal offense. The data is provided merely for illustrative and discussion purposes. Performance data using a wide variety of time periods is provided. Rather than focusing on the specific time periods used or the results derived, the reader should focus instead on the underlying principles.

None of the material presented here is intended to serve as the basis for any financial decision, nor does any of the information contained within constitute an offer to buy or sell any security. Such an offer is made only by prospectus, which you should read carefully before investing or sending money.

The material presented in this book is accurate to the best of my knowledge. However, performance data changes over time, and laws frequently change as well, and my advice could change accordingly. Therefore, the reader is encouraged to verify the status of such information before acting.

While all the stories and anecdotes recited here are true, all of the names have been changed to protect each individual's privacy. It is impossible to ascertain the identity of any person based solely on the information in this book.

For Ruchie

Contents

Preface

"I'm proud to have chosen a profession that challenges my intelligence and allows me at the end of every day to know that I have significantly helped my clients."

Jerald L. Aloof, RFC
Financial Advisor

I love helping people. Being a Financial Advisor has given me a unique opportunity to help people in one of the most important aspects of their lives. Since I specialize in retirement planning, the role I play in my clients' lives is all the more significant.

I began my career with EF Hutton & Co. in Lower Manhattan in 1986. I've been involved in practically every aspect of investing from trading commodity futures to being named Branch-Office Insurance Coordinator while at Dean Witter Reynolds in 1990. It was that same year that I teamed up with partner, David Mattos; together, we decided to focus our practice in the area of retirement planning. In 1991 we were both named Associate Vice President—Investments and Retirement Planning Specialists. In 1993 we moved to PaineWebber and started presenting our very popular retirement planning seminars. While at PaineWebber, we were named Vice Presidents—Investments and Retirement Planning Consultants.

For the last number of years, I've wanted to take what I've learned in my years in this business and put them together in a manual of sorts; this very useful, albeit brief volume is the culmination of that effort. "Rolling Over" can be an invaluable tool to the individual investor. It covers the basics of Investing, Retirement Planning, Estate Planning and Asset Allocation—and, it goes slightly beyond the basics. It is an excellent resource for both the new investor and the seasoned individual investor.

This book is not meant as a do-it-yourself retirement planning manual. It is intended to familiarize the reader with many of the aspects of investing, retirement planning and estate planning. In estate planning, retirement planning and investing, as in all-important matters in life, one is strongly urged to seek the counsel of a qualified advisor.

Thank You

To Al-mighty G-D for all the wonderful gifts you've given me in my life. To my wonderful wife and soul mate, Ruchie—I wouldn't be half of what I am without you. To my great kids: Shaynde, Daniella, Dovie, Goldie, Moshe and Elleonna—you make life worth living. To my parents for setting my feet on the road to success. To my clients—You're the reason I come to work each day. To everyone who's helped me along the way in my career. And last, but certainly not least, to my partner, Dave—Onward and Upward!

PART I

General Financial Planning

How Can Financial Planning Help?

Think of your financial situation as your personal corporation. If you were given a chance to buy stock in yourself, would you do it? A company's annual report includes certain financial statements giving an indication of how solid or shaky the company's financial situation might be. There are tools that tell you about your own personal financial situation as well.

Corporations and individuals want to know the following: How do assets such as property, stocks, mutual funds, money markets, cash, etc. stack up against the loans they have? How did their income and expenses balance last year? What type of plan, if any, do they have for this year? How have they projected their income and expenses so they continually monitor their plans?

If you haven't done any of the above, you are not unusual. Most people operate on the checkbook system. If there is money, spend it. If there isn't—well, now what?

Yet, despite current expenses, you need to look ahead to the time when your earned income will stop due to retirement. You want to feel that if you must stop or choose to stop working, you will be financially secure.

Financial Planning can help in a number of ways. It can:

- Provide a realistic picture of the money you will actually need at the time you wish to retire.

- Help you to make more beneficial use of your current income and savings.

- Combat the effects of inflation on your savings.

- Push you to take advantage of savings options that exist now, but may not be available later.

- Identify the expected sources and amounts of your retirement income.

What's An "Investment"?

In simple language, an investment is an outlay of money to produce income or profit. Unfortunately, this definition fails to clear up much of the confusion about the where, when and why of investing. You owe it to yourself to find out what investment options are available so that you can make well calculated and educated choices about what will be best for you.

All of us are investors of one sort or another. Some invest through savings bonds, some through an account at the local bank or credit union, or equity gained by buying a home. Others put money into stocks, bonds, mutual funds or similar investments.

Though we are all investors, many of us are not getting as much as we can out of our investments. Perhaps we have questions about certain types of investments, such as, *"Are they really safe?"* and *"Can they produce the types of returns we need to meet our goals?"*

These are realistic concerns that sometimes cause us to stay away from good investment opportunities.

The key to making yourself financially successful is to gain some understanding of the alternatives available to you. By first reading up on basic terminology and investing concepts, you'll be in a better position to understand and evaluate your options.

So-called financial experts may include someone at your local bank, a benefit specialist with your employer or union, insurance agent, savings and loan officer, credit union manager and so on. While they can be good sources of information, their recommendations or information should never automatically become your decisions. Keep asking questions and getting information until you feel you understand the facts, then you will feel confident to make educated choices. A wise investor should always consult a qualified Financial Advisor as the ultimate source of financial advice and recommendations.

Different Asset Classes

In today's investment universe full of uncertainties, allocating your investment among asset classes such as stocks, bonds and cash isn't quite as simple as it once was. Stocks and bonds are now broken out into various asset classes, each with their own risk/return profile that you must take into consideration before investing. Don't let the various asset classes scare you off. The key to remember with asset classes is that they may help to improve your investment portfolio performance while keeping your risk at a level you feel comfortable with.

For the purpose of asset allocation, there are three major asset classes—stocks, bonds, and cash. Stocks, which represent a share of ownership in a business, are essential to long-term investment planning because historically they increase in value. Traditionally, bonds have been seen as fixed-income-producing investments because the interest they pay is typically fixed. Bonds also play an important role in balancing movement in the stock market and in providing a cushion against stock market volatility. Cash and cash equivalents, such as U.S. Treasury bills and money markets, offer safety and liquidity for money that might be needed within a relatively short time frame.

Since each of these three types of assets respond differently to shifts in the economy and markets, spreading money among stocks, bonds, and cash equivalents can help investors ride out market uncertainty.

Stocks

Stock is an equity investment that represents part ownership in a corporation and entitles you to part of that corporation's earnings and assets. Common stocks give shareholders voting rights but no guarantee of dividend payments. Preferred stocks provide no voting rights but usually guarantee a dividend payment. In the past, shareholders received a paper stock certificate—called a security—verifying the number of shares they owned. Today, share ownership is usually recorded electronically, and the shares are held in "street name" by your brokerage firm.

There are two types of equity or stock asset classes: Domestic (U.S.) and International.

Domestic

The domestic asset class includes Large-cap stocks, Mid-cap stocks and Small-cap stocks. Of course, many investment professionals narrow these down even further, but we'll stick to the basics. Large-cap, Mid-cap and Small-cap, are abbreviations for Large Capitalization, Mid Capitalization and Small Capitalization. The market capitalization of a company is calculated by multiplying its stock price by the number of shares outstanding.

For example, a company has 8 million shares outstanding with a price of $100 per share. The market capitalization of that company is $800 million. 8,000,000 x $100 = $800,000,000. Would this company be considered a Large-Cap, Mid-Cap or Small-Cap? Well, that depends on whom you ask.

There is no common definition of capitalization levels to classify stocks. Generally, capitalization is broken out as follows: Large Caps—$6 Billion and up, Mid Caps—$2 billion to $6 billion, and Small Caps—up to $2 billion.

Understanding what determines if a stock is Large-, Mid- or Small-Cap is step one. Step two is knowing about the risks and potential returns each offers, so that you can make an investment decision based on your financial needs and goals.

International

International equities are generally riskier than domestic equities but can also have better growth potential. Risks uniquely associated with international investing include varying securities regulations, political and social instability and currency rate fluctuations. International stocks, however, add a key ingredient to any portfolio—diversification.

The U.S. equity market didn't fair quite so well as compared to other countries during the '70's and '80's. In fact, according to the Morgan Stanley Capital International Index (MSCI) since 1978, five countries had better average annual equity returns than the U.S.

Additionally, 2/3's of the 30,000+ stocks are outside the U.S. and contain over half of the world's market capitalization. Some of the biggest and best-known companies, such as Sony Corp (Japan), are foreign companies. Finally, as the global economy expands, many emerging markets are growing faster and have better growth potential than the U.S., which can mean great growth potential for your portfolio.

As a general rule, if you are 10 or more years from retirement, you should focus on growth investments such as stocks and stock mutual funds. These investments have the greatest potential to boost the value of your retirement accounts. In order to reduce risk, more conservative investors may elect to invest a portion of assets in bond funds, which do not tend to fluctuate as much in price as do stock funds.

Growth versus Value Companies

Introduction

There has been an ongoing debate for many years as to whether higher stock market returns can be achieved by investing for "growth" or by investing for "value." There is one simple fact "valuation begins and ends with profits." Just about everybody agrees with that. The faster a company's earnings grow and the more reliable they are, the more investors will pay for its stock. When it comes to strategy, though, Wall Street is decidedly less single-minded. Everybody wants to buy low and sell high, but how low is low and how high is high? The purpose of this section is to answer this major question.

Generally, the Street is divided between two camps: Growth and Value. Growth investors believe in buying stocks with above-average earnings growth no matter what the price. Value investors look exclusively for "bargains," or stocks that are trading at a discount to their usual valuation. In another words, "Investing for "value" means purchasing stocks at relatively low prices, as indicated by low price-to-earnings (P/E), price-to-book, price-to-sales ratios and high dividend yields. Investing for "growth" results in just the opposite—high price-to-earnings, price-to-book, price-to-sales ratios and low dividend yields.

Let's explain this in more detail: "Growth" investors are more apt to subscribe to the "efficient market hypothesis" which maintains that the current market price of a stock reflects all the currently "knowable" information about a company and, so, is the most reasonable price for that stock at that given point in time. They seek to enjoy their rewards by participating in what the growth of the underlying company imparts to the growth of the price of its stock.

"Value" investors, by contrast, put more weight on their judgments about the extent to which they think a stock is mispriced in the marketplace. If a stock is under priced, it is a good buy; if it is overpriced, it is a good sell. It is as simple as that. They seek to enjoy their rewards by buying stocks that are depressed because their companies are going through periods of difficulty; riding their prices upward and selling them when their price objectives are reached.

You are probably asking yourself, "Which strategy shows the better returns?" Well, the answer to that question depends, in part, upon the periods over which they are compared. It has, however, been my impression (based upon facts and figures), over the past several decades, that "value" investing has received the more hype. Frankly speaking, there's no right answer, when it comes to decide which strategy makes the most sense—people make money in both ways. But there are several reasons why we think a value approach is superior, particularly for long-term investors.

First of all, history shows that when you buy stocks that are cheap relative to others your returns benefit over time. It's easy to see why. Suppose you're looking at a stock that typically trades in a P/E range between 20 and 30. If you buy it at 20 and let it move up to 29 before you sell, you clearly see a bigger profit than if you buy at 27, let it move up to 30, and then sell when it starts to head back down. Even if you ignore short-term cycles and hold for the long term, you're better off if you buy the stock as cheaply as possible in the first place.

The danger, of course, is that your company has problems that justify its low valuation. What if it stays at 20 and holds your money hostage? That's something growth investors rarely have to worry about. But if you choose companies that are in good financial shape and there's an explanation for why their stock is selling cheap, chances are the shares will resume their growth eventually; and if they don't budge off the bottom, you really haven't lost much. That isn't true if your exit timings are not correct from a volatile high-multiple stock and you get caught in a downdraft.

In my view the ideal stock, of course, will have a low P/E and a rapid rate of earnings growth. But unfortunately, such situations are rare, since any whiff of growth attracts investors and boosts the price. But that doesn't mean there aren't times when a stock like Microsoft or Cisco Systems is selling at a much lower price than it should; you just have to be ready to pounce. And that's really the point. Above all else, we believe investors should be opportunistic as they set out to build a balanced portfolio of stocks. You shouldn't miss the opportunity to own big, important companies like Microsoft or Wal-Mart. But remember, you shouldn't pay too much for them either.

Performance and Safety Aspects in Investments

One of the most fascinating aspects of the current mutual fund craze is the buying public's utter disregard for the quality of the investments in the portfolios of the mutual funds it acquires. It is almost universally accepted that, if Fund A has gone up more than Fund B over some period of time, it is a better-managed fund. How that performance was achieved tends to take a back seat to the performance numbers themselves.

How performance is achieved, however, can be of critical importance. The reason it can be important is that the stock market is fickle and, when it falls apart, it falls apart without warning. If a portfolio has achieved its perform-ance by owning high-risk securities (e.g., small, less liquid companies with large amounts of debt, operating in highly cyclical, rapidly changing, or highly competitive industries) and/or using high-risk strategies (e.g., derivative secu-rities such as options, futures, or warrants), it is not well-prepared for those difficult times which unexpectedly rock the securities markets about every quarter of a century or so.

Premiums for Safety

Let us recognize that we are naturally predisposed to pay a premium for safety. We stop and look both ways before we cross the street, in spite of the extra expenditure of time and energy it requires. We carry fire insurance on our houses, in spite of the improbability that our houses will burn down, and in spite of the many other things we might otherwise enjoy with all the money we pay for insurance premiums.

United States Treasury Securities are considered to be the world's safest invest-ments; however, securities of agencies of the United States Government are not far behind. Federal Land Bank, Federal Farm Credit Bank, Federal Home Loan Bank, Federal Home Loan Mortgage, and Federal National Mortgage Association bonds all carry Moody's ratings of Aaa. The former are considered safer because they are "legal" obligations of the United States Government, whereas the latter are only "moral" obligations of the United States Government. (The solvency of the Federal Deposit Insurance Corporation, which insures our bank accounts, for example, is backed by a "moral," as opposed to a "legal," obligation of the U. S. Government.)

Try to contemplate a scenario in which the United States Government fulfills its obligations to pay interest and principal on its legal obligations but permits the obligations of its federal agencies (including FDIC insurance) to default. This, it would seem, would need to be an event more catastrophic than our republic has yet experienced, and certainly an event more serious even than the Great Depression of the 1930s.

Nevertheless, the marketplace pays a premium to own U. S. Treasuries, as opposed to Federal Agency bonds. A glance at the Wall Street Journal reveals that, for comparable maturities, bond buyers are willing to sacrifice between 1/2 of 1% and 1% in yield to own the former, rather than the latter. As improb-able as it is that the incremental safety afforded by Treasuries over Federal

Agencies will ever be needed, investors are willing to pay a substantial premium (sacrifice in yield) to own them.

The same situation exists with municipal bonds. In spite of the fact that the general obligations (GOs) of a state are backed by the taxing power of all of the assets within that state, Aaa state GOs yield less than Aa state GOs. The differential between Aaa corporate bonds and Aa corporates provides still another example. The sacrifice in yield required to own an Aaa corporate versus a Aa corporate is of the order of 1/2 of 1%. Again, imagine the economic or monetary scenario in which Aaa corporate America meets its obligations, but Aa corporate America defaults.

Given that municipal bonds are considered less safe than U. S. Government bonds, that corporate bonds are considered less safe than municipal bonds, and that a company's common stock is always less safe than its weakest bond, should we not expect that the marketplace might be willing to pay a premium for safety (as well as for appreciation potential) in a common stock?

The important principle to understand is that, given two common stock portfolios, X and Y, if Portfolio X is made up of higher quality issues—companies less apt than those in Portfolio Y to go bankrupt in a period such as the Great Depression of the 1930s, the Great Credit Crunch of the 1970s, or an economic/monetary scenario more catastrophic than has yet been experienced—then, barring the occurrence of such a catastrophic event, and all other things being equal, Portfolio X should show a lesser return than Portfolio Y. Portfolio X must pay an insurance premium for its added protection against catastrophic events, as improbable as their realization may seem. It should expect to pay this premium by accepting lesser total returns, in the absence of a catastrophic event.

New Morningstar Data

The Morningstar mutual fund service is the most popular and most comprehensive of all the mutual fund rating services. Beginning in late 1996 and early 1997, the service modified the way it categorized mutual funds. Common stock funds are now divided into nine groups, according to whether they invest in large capitalization, medium capitalization, or small capitalization companies, and whether their investment styles are predominantly "growth" oriented, "value" oriented, or a "blend" of the two. For the first time, this data gives us an opportunity more easily to study, compare, and contrast the collective character of the portfolios, and the performance records, of large numbers of mutual funds using "growth" and "value" stock approaches as their invest-ment strategies.

The data used for this analysis covers over twelve hundred mutual funds with over $1/2 trillion in assets. Morningstar makes such an analysis relatively easy because it publishes a page for each investment style, which it calls an "Overview." On this page is a listing of the twenty-five largest holdings of all the mutual funds in each sector, the relative size of each position, and the col-lective performance data for the funds in that sector. By examining the quality of the twenty-five largest holdings of the mutual funds in a sector, we can get a pretty good picture of the character of the portfolios in that sector.

Quality and Safety Measurement of Large-Cap Portfolios

The most popular, and probably the best, way to measure the safety of a com-mon stock is to look at its Standard & Poor's rating. Standard & Poor's rates most large capitalization stocks, and a portion of the universe of mid-cap and small-cap stocks, on a scale of A+, A, A-, B+, B, B-, C, and D. These ratings are in no way meant by Standard & Poor's to be prognostications of performance in normal markets. They are meant more to serve as measures of the degrees of protection available in each security in a catastrophic market.

Based upon the twenty-five largest holdings in the collective portfolios of the large capitalization "growth" and large capitalization "value" sectors, a profile of each sector appears in the following table:

Large-Cap Style	S&P Quality Rating At or Above		
	A+	A	A-
Growth	29.5%	34.4%	42.6%
Value	19.0%	22.8%	32.6%

An alternative measure of the ability of a company to withstand economic and/or monetary adversity can be found in its Value Line "financial strength" rating. This is essentially an assessment of the company's balance sheet. Value Line's rating scale is as follows: A++, A+, A, B++, B+, B, C++, C+, and C.

A breakdown of the financial strength ratings for the large-cap "growth" and "value" portfolios appears in the following table:

	VL Financial Strength Rating at or Above		
Large-Cap Style	A++	A+	A
Growth	37.5%	61.2%	86.4%
Value	13.7%	45.2%	73.3%

The implication appears to be that, at least for large capitalization portfolios, the quality is conspicuously higher, and so the safety significantly greater, in "growth" style portfolios than in "value" style portfolios.

Such a finding should not be surprising. "Growth" stocks represent companies that are currently thriving, while "value" stocks commonly represent companies in trouble. That is why the prices of the former are high and the prices of the latter are low. Companies that are thriving are apt to be in better shape to confront catastrophic conditions than are companies already in trouble, even before a catastrophe occurs.

Let us state again, however, that, for this incremental quality and safety, "growth" investors should expect to pay some price—such as the acceptance of a lower total return on their portfolios in normal times than they might enjoy if they were to sacrifice some of their quality and safety as in "value" investing.

The Records of Performance

The inference, so far, is that, because "growth" investors enjoy greater protection against such perils as another Great Depression, they should expect, and should be satisfied with, lesser rates of return in normal times than those presumably enjoyed by "value" investors. To compare the rates of return of higher-quality "growth" portfolios with the rates of return of lower-quality "value" portfolios, in normal times, as we have said, is to compare "apples to oranges."

Though it may appear that "growth" investors should be content with lesser returns than those enjoyed by "value" investors, before reaching the conclusion that they actually do receive lesser returns, let us examine the following data—again from Morningstar:

	Relative Annualized 10-Year Total Returns		
Comparison	Large-Cap	Mid-Cap	Small-Cap
Growth vs. Value	+2.85%	+2.79%	+2.95%
Growth vs. Blend	+1.67%	+0.98%	+1.84%

As can be seen, whether the "growth" strategy is compared against the "value" strategy or a "blend" of "growth" and "value" strategies, over the past ten years, the "growth" strategy has produced the higher returns. Furthermore, depending upon whether we are looking at small-cap, mid-cap, or large-cap portfolios, this out-performance of "growth" over "value" or "blend" strategies has ranged from nearly 1% to nearly 3% per year.

Conclusion

Each investor has to decide what level of risk tolerance they're comfortable with. Whether the decision is made to be aggressive or conservative, it's the growth and the value stocks that can make the difference. After discussing this topic in details from various angles, we can safely conclude that "growth" investors enjoy higher total returns than "value" investors, and that they also have greater protection against shattering events such as depressions, credit crunches, and other catastrophes such as we can only imagine. For these benefits, however, growth investors must be willing to accept a greater portion of their total returns in the form of irregular capital gains, as opposed to more regular dividends; and they must be willing to accept higher short-term volatility in the values of their portfolios.

Bonds

Bonds are debt securities issued by corporations and governments. Bonds are, in fact, loans that you and other investors make to the issuers in return for the promise of being paid interest, usually but not always at a fixed rate. The issuer also promises to repay the debt on time and in full. Because most bonds pay interest on a regular basis, they are also described as fixed-income investments.

There are two general types of bond asset classes: Taxable and Tax-free.

Taxable Bonds

Taxable Bonds are given a credit rating based upon an analysis of the issuers' financial condition, revenue sources securing the bond and other factors from various rating agencies such as Moody's, Standard and Poor's and Fitch (formerly Duff & Phelps). Investment grade bonds have more favorable credit ratings and non-investment grade bonds have less favorable credit ratings. Investment grade bonds are considered less risky than non-investment grade bonds and therefore, just like with other types of investments, tend to produce lower returns over the long-term than riskier investments. Non-investment grade bonds, which have lower credit ratings and are therefore more speculative, tend to produce higher returns over the long-term.

Tax-Free Bonds

Tax-free municipal bonds (often called "munis") are debt securities issued by various cities, states and municipalities throughout the United States. As such, they are given special tax-free status. If you live in, say, Indiana, and buy an Indianapolis muni, you will pay no federal, state, and, in many cases, local taxes on the interest you receive. But before you start dreaming of an IRS-free life, let's take a closer look. First, tax-free bonds usually come with a lower interest rate—after all, you get to keep all of it. But how do you know that you won't come out ahead buying a higher interest rate bond and paying the taxes?

How to Decide Between a Taxable or Tax-Free Bond?

This is not that hard a decision to make. You simply convert the regular bond's interest rate to its equivalent "after-tax rate" and compare that with the tax-free bond's interest rate—it's that simple; whichever is larger, wins.

To find the after-tax rate, first you add up your marginal income tax rates. If you are in the 15% bracket for federal income taxes and pay 4% in state taxes, your marginal tax rate is 19%. If you are in the 28% federal bracket and your state taxes are 7%, your marginal tax rate is 35%. Now you have to find the reciprocal of your marginal tax rate. Just subtract from 1. The reciprocal of 19% (0.19) would be 0.81; the reciprocal of 35% (0.35) would be 0.65. Now you can convert any interest rate to its after-tax equivalent.

Say you were considering buying a new issue corporate (taxable) bond with a coupon rate of 8%. The after-tax equivalent for someone in the 19% bracket is 6.48% (8% x 0.81), but for someone in the 35% tax bracket, the after-tax equivalent rate is 5.2% (8% x 0.65).

So, for someone in the lower tax bracket, the tax-free bond would have to beat 6.48% to be a good deal, but for someone in the higher bracket, the tax-free bond would only have to beat 5.2%.

It works in reverse, too. To see how a tax-free bond compares to a taxable bond, divide the tax-free interest rate by your tax rate. A tax-free bond paying 5% would be equivalent to a taxable interest rate of 7.69% for someone with a marginal tax rate of 35% (5/.65= 7.69), but only equivalent to 6.17% for someone with a marginal rate of 19% (5/.81=6.17).

In general, tax-free bonds are usually only attractive to persons in the upper income brackets.

As you near and then enter retirement, you'll need to balance your expectations for growth with your need for capital preservation. Investing a portion of your retirement plan assets in money market or bond funds can help you maintain a more stable investment value for the portion of your investment you expect to draw on in the near future. But don't forget that your retirement could last 20 years or more. You will likely need to continue to invest a portion of your assets in stocks and stock mutual funds, which can help you stay ahead of inflation.

Cash

Cash is the third and final major asset class. Cash and cash equivalents, such as money market accounts are considered "safe" investments, but have virtually no growth potential. The Financial Accounting Standards Board (FASB), which is responsible for establishing national accounting standards, defines cash equivalents as highly liquid securities with maturities of less than three months. Liquid securities typically are those that can be sold easily with little or no loss of value.

Understanding the various asset classes and sub-classes can help you decide how to diversify your portfolio. By knowing the associated risks and growth potential each asset class and sub-class has to offer, you can diversify your investment portfolio in a manner that best suits your financial objectives while keeping your risk exposure at a level you are comfortable with.

Mutual Funds

One way to further diversify your investments, while also using an asset alloca-tion strategy, is to invest in mutual funds. These investments, by design, are broadly diversified within specific asset classes and generally actively managed by experienced investment professionals. Mutual funds are available in a broad array of asset classes, such as stocks and bonds, making them excellent choices for any investor's portfolio.

Few people have the time, knowledge, resources and money to successfully build and manage a portfolio of individual stocks, bonds, and other invest-ments. That's why millions of Americans have chosen mutual funds as the foundation on which to build their investment strategy.

Mutual funds pool the money of many people and invest it in a portfolio of stocks, bonds, and/or money market instruments to meet a specific investment objective. Full-time, professional money managers manage mutual funds. As an investor, you receive shares of the mutual fund in exchange for your invest-ment dollars.

General Classifications of Mutual Funds

Mutual funds can be classified into four broad categories:

- Money Market Funds—appropriate if you are investing for a short period of time and desire capital preservation. Money market funds invest in high-quality, short-term securities.[1]

- Income Funds—appropriate if you have a need for current income. Income funds invest in bonds, both corporate and government, hav-ing a range of average maturities.

- Growth and Income Funds—appropriate when you are seeking current income along with potential long-term growth. Growth and income funds generally invest in both bonds and dividend paying stocks.

- Growth Funds—appropriate if you seek long-term growth potential. Growth funds generally invest the majority of their assets in stocks.

---

[1] Money market funds are neither insured nor guaranteed by the Federal Deposit Insurance Corporation or any other government agency.

Mutual funds are designed to meet your diverse investment needs. Within each category you will find a range of investment objectives. There is no guarantee, however, that your particular mutual fund will meet its investment objective. When you're considering a mutual fund, be sure to consult with your Financial Advisor.

Most Common Benefits of Mutual Funds

Mutual funds provide you with an attractive, cost-effective alternative to direct purchases of stocks or bonds—you don't need to be wealthy to invest in them. Mutual funds offer you a number of benefits including:

- Diversification
- Professional Management
- Liquidity
- Flexibility
- Convenience

Moreover, as a shareholder, you also generally receive easy-to-read account statements detailing information on account values, share transactions, and dividend and capital gains distributions.

Annuities

Annuities can be a key component of your overall retirement savings plan. Annuities enable you to save money on a tax-deferred basis, so all of your money can work for you now. No taxes are due until you begin to withdraw your money, which can be years later.

When you're ready to receive income, generally in retirement, annuities can provide you with a variety of income choices, including a guaranteed income that you can never outlive. In addition, if you die before income payments begin, many variable annuities provide a death benefit that guarantees your beneficiaries will never receive less than the amount contributed to the contract, less any withdrawals or fees. In recent years, many insurance companies have added a "stepped-up" death benefit option, which automatically locks in the highest anniversary value of variable annuities as a death benefit. There are also a plethora of new living income benefits as well. When considering investing in annuities, it is essential that you work with a Financial Advisor as the options are numerous and can get overwhelming.

Types of Annuities

There are two primary types of annuities. One is a **deferred annuity**, a type of long-term personal retirement account, which allows you to save and invest on a tax-deferred basis with an option to receive a stream of income at a later date. The other is an **immediate annuity**, which provides regular income payments right away or within a short time afterward. Keep in mind that deferred annuities are long-term vehicles. Withdrawals of earnings from a deferred annuity are subject to ordinary income tax and may be subject to contract withdrawal charges. Because deferred annuities are designed specifically for retirement, withdrawals made before age 59½ are generally subject to a 10% tax penalty.

Deferred Annuity

A deferred annuity is a type of personal retirement account that allows you to grow your assets on a tax-deferred basis for long-term goals, like retirement. There are two phases to a deferred annuity: the saving and investing phase, when your assets are invested for potential growth, and the retirement income phase, when you can choose how and when to receive income. There are two types of deferred annuities: fixed deferred annuities and variable deferred annuities. Fixed annuities generally offer lower risk and lower growth potential, while variable annuities can offer greater growth potential in return for increased risk.

Fixed Annuities

Fixed annuities pay a fixed, guaranteed rate of interest. The issuing company guarantees the rates for a specified time period. At the end of that period, the issuing company will reset a new, guaranteed rate. The interest rate and time period vary depending on the annuity contract. Most contracts have a guaranteed minimum interest rate.

Variable Annuities

Variable annuities offer more growth potential in return for a higher level of risk. Variable annuities can offer investment choice and flexibility through a variety of professionally managed investment portfolios. These portfolios generally include stock and bond portfolios, ranging from conservative to aggressive risk levels. The value of a variable annuity will fluctuate, depending on how the investment options perform. It is important to note that today's variable annuities offer significant death benefits, such as minimum anniversary date stepped-up values, which guarantee the annuitant's beneficiaries the highest anniversary date value. Certain companies will also offer a guaranteed percentage return on the original contract value as a death benefit. In addition, many insurance companies offer significant living benefits, which guarantee the investors principal or assure a percentage return should the investor wish to annuitize the contract. The investor is urged to discuss the various variable annuity options with a qualified financial advisor.

Immediate Annuity

An immediate annuity is an annuity contract that you generally buy with a lump sum and from which you begin receiving income within a short period, always less than 13 months. An immediate annuity can be either fixed or variable. The key difference is that a deferred annuity is a long-term vehicle, designed to accumulate assets over time. When you are ready to receive income, usually at retirement, you can convert your savings to a steady stream of income that meets your needs. Immediate annuities are designed to begin making annuity payments right away or within a short time afterward. In addition, deferred annuities may be purchased with a lump sum or multiple contributions.

Diversification of Assets

Before explaining the diversification of assets, let's understand clearly that many people commonly confuse the terms asset allocation and diversification. While asset allocation refers to the different asset classes (equity, bonds, and cash), diversification refers to the process of further dividing your investment dollars within each of the three asset classes. So, allocating a portion of your investments in each asset class to appropriate sub-categories can further reduce risk and enhance return.

For example, you might decide to achieve diversification in the stock asset class by choosing both domestic and international stocks. If you choose to invest in mutual funds, you might diversify your holdings by investing in funds classified as "growth and income," "growth," and "aggressive growth." Similarly, you can achieve diversity in your bond portfolio by selecting different types of bonds with different maturity dates and by using bond mutual funds. With diversification, setbacks in one investment can be offset by gains in another.

How Diversification Lowers Risk

Diversification is a risk-management technique that mixes a wide variety of investments within a portfolio in order to minimize the impact that any one security will have on the overall performance of the portfolio. Diversification lowers the risk of your portfolio. In financial language, over time and through bull and bear markets, a sector-diversified portfolio earns higher returns with lower risk than a non-diversified portfolio. Academics have complex formulas to demonstrate how this works, but before examining some of these, let's look at an example:

Say you live on an island where the entire economy consists of only two companies: one sells umbrellas while the other sells sunscreen. If you invest your entire portfolio in the company that sells umbrellas, you'll have strong performance during the rainy season, but poor performance when it's sunny outside. The reverse occurs with the sunscreen company, the alternative investment: your portfolio will perform well when the sun is out, but it will tank when the clouds roll in. Chances are you'd rather have constant, steady returns. The solution is to invest 50% in one company and 50% in the other. Since you have diversified your portfolio, you will get decent performance year round instead of, depending on the season, having either excellent or terrible performance. Similarly, by diversifying your portfolio in many other investments you are likely to reduce the risks considerably.

There are three main practices that can help you ensure the best diversification:

- Spread your portfolio among multiple investment vehicles such as cash, stocks, bonds, mutual funds, and perhaps even some real estate.

- Vary the risk in your securities. You're not restricted to choosing only blue chip stocks. In fact, it would be wise to pick investments with varied risk levels; this will ensure that gains in other investments offset large losses.

- Vary your securities by industry. This will minimize the impact of specific risks of certain industries.

Diversification is the most important component in helping you reach your long-range financial goals while minimizing your risk. At the same time, diversification is not an ironclad guarantee or foolproof method against loss. No matter how much diversification you employ, investing involves taking on some sort of risk. Experts say, "The Biggest Risk in Life Is Not to Take Any Risk". So, be prepared to take some risk, but remember it should be well calculated.

Asset Correlation & Covariance

Asset Correlation measures the extent to which the returns on two assets move together (i.e. the extent to which those returns behave similarly in response to market events or stimuli). Correlation and Covariance measure the extent to which the returns on two assets move together.

We want to split our investments between two asset classes, A and B, say Large Cap and Small Cap stocks.

Assume the Average Annual Returns for each asset are "a" and "b" where a 12.3% return means a = 0.123 and so on. If a fraction x of our portfolio is devoted to asset A, and the balance, 1-x, is devoted to asset B, then G, the Mean Return for our portfolio will be

(1) $G = a x + b (1-x)$

You would rebalance your portfolio every year, in order to maintain the x and (1-x) fractions.

If the Standard Deviations for each asset are P and Q, respectively, then SD, the Standard Deviation for our portfolio is given by:

(2) $SD2 = P^2 x^2 + Q^2 (1-x)^2 + 2 x (1-x) R$

Where R is the Covariance between the two assets, A and B.

If the annual returns of asset A, over N years, are $a_1, a_2, a_3 \dots a_N$ then, for this asset:

Mean Return $= a = (1/N) \sum a_n$
(Standard Deviation) $^2 = P^2 = (1/N) \sum (a_n - a)^2$

Let's see the Covariance.

Covariance $= R = (1/N) \sum (a_n - a) (b_n - b)$

Where:

b_n stands for the annual returns of asset B; and

$(a_n - a)$ and $(b_n - b)$ are the deviations from the average returns.

If the two assets were correlated, then when the first return is larger (or smaller) than its average it's likely that the second return is larger (or smaller) than its average and the product $(a_n - a)(b_n - b)$ is more likely to be positive so adding all these terms is likely give a positive sum.

However, when they are NOT correlated, it's likely to be ZERO, the positive deviations canceling with the negative. Let's see in the picture below to understand it:

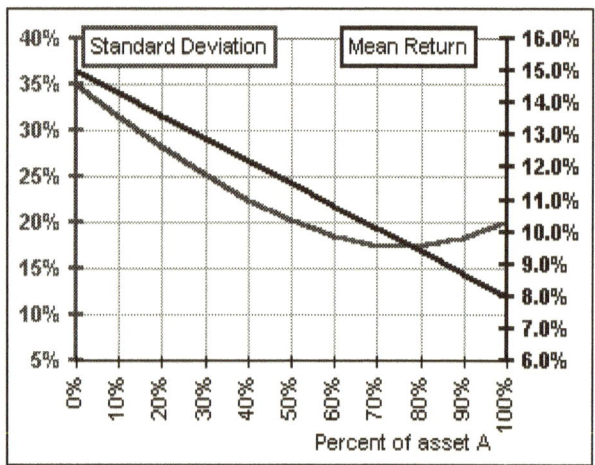

It assumes that asset A has a Mean Return $a = 8\%$ and a Standard Deviation $P = 20\%$ and asset B has Mean $b = 15\%$ and Standard Deviation $Q = 35\%$ and we assume no correlation between asset classes and we devote a certain percentage of our portfolio to asset A and look at the Mean Return and Standard Deviation of our portfolio using the magic formulas (1) and (2) above, with $R = 0$.

If your objective is to minimize the Volatility (or Standard Deviation) then a combination of two uncorrelated assets is better than 100% of either.

Most people are more interested in Annualized Return than Standard Deviation. Let's use the following approximation for AR the Annualized Portfolio Return:

$AR = G - SD^2/2$ in terms of G, the Mean Portfolio Return, and SD, the Portfolio Standard Deviation:

(3)   AR = a x + b (1-x) - (1/2){P² x² + Q² (1-x) ² + 2 x (1-x) R}

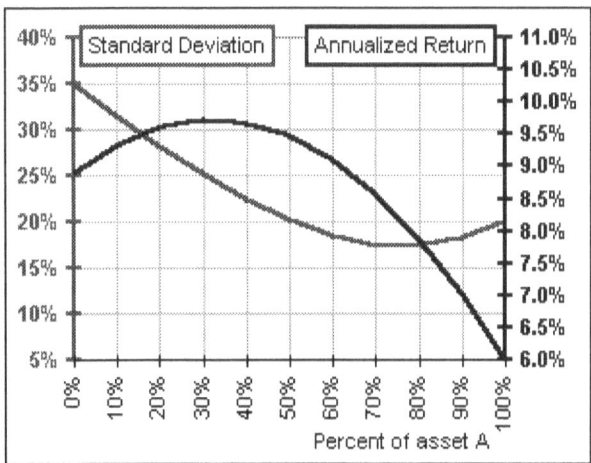

Here it's again assumed that asset A has a Mean Return a = 8% and a Standard Deviation P = 20% and asset B has Mean b = 15% and Standard Deviation Q = 35% and we again assume no correlation between asset classes.

So it is evident that a combination is again better than either.

This example shows no correlation. However, we'd want more of asset A if we want a smaller volatility, since asset A has the smaller volatility; on the other hand, the more of asset B in the portfolio, the greater the gain because asset B has the larger Mean Return.

Of course the problem is that there is another effect that works in the opposite direction: if you limit yourself to low-risk securities, you'll be limiting yourself to investments that tend to have low rates of return. So what you really want to do is include some higher growth, higher risk securities in your portfolio, and combine them in a smart way, so that some of their fluctuations cancel each other out. (In statistical terms, you're looking for a combined standard deviation that's low, relative to the standard deviations of the individual securities.) The result should give you a high average rate of return, with less of the harmful fluctuations.

Here's a set of Portfolio assets where we assume a Correlation Coefficient from r = -1.0 (meaning when one return goes up, the other goes down, in perfect synchronism) to r = +1.0 (meaning when one return goes up, the other goes up as well).

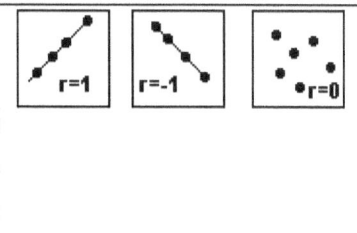

The **Pearson Correlation Coefficient, r,** is related to the **Covariance** like so:

$$\text{Covariance} = r\, P\, Q$$

Here are some further examples of correlation:

Asset **A** has a Mean Return a = 8% and a Standard Deviation P = 20% and asset **B** has Mean b = 15% and Standard Deviation Q = 35%:

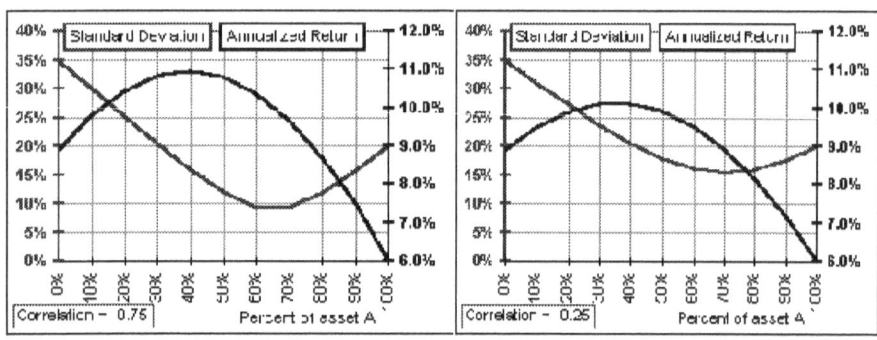

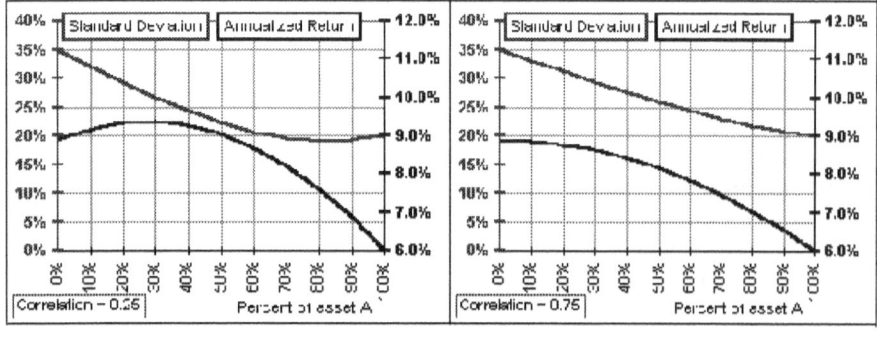

Let's see the formula for getting the **Maximum** Annualized Return.

Maximum Annualized Return (*approximately*), obtained for :
$$x = (1/2) + (1/2) \{ Q^2 - P^2 + 2(a - b) \} / \{ P^2 + Q^2 - 2r\,P\,Q \}$$

Where:
a and **P** are the Mean Annual Return and Standard Deviation for asset **A**
b and **Q** are the Mean Annual Return and Standard Deviation for asset **B**
r = **Covariance**/(**PQ**) is the Pearson Correlation Coefficient

If you find the above formula a bit tedious, you can use this simple calculation to get the "Optimal" parameters (yielding the largest Annualized Return):

$$(1+\text{Annualized\_Return})^2 = (1+\text{Mean\_Return})^2 - \text{Standard\_Deviation}^2$$

Remember here a ≠ b and P ≠ Q and r ≠ 1

Asset Allocation

Throughout history common stocks have outperformed most financial instruments. If an investor plans to have an investment for a long period of time, then their portfolio should be comprised mostly of stocks; however, investors who don't have this kind of time should diversify their portfolios.

Asset allocation is an investment portfolio technique that aims to balance risk and create diversification by dividing assets among major categories such as bonds, stocks, real estate, and cash. Each asset class has different levels of return and risk, so each will behave differently over time in different situations. At the same time that one asset is increasing in value; another may be decreasing, or not increasing as much.

The underlying principle of asset allocation is that the older a person gets, the less risk he or she should face. After you retire you may have to depend on your savings as your only source of income; you should, therefore, invest more conservatively.

Determining the proper mix of investments in your portfolio is extremely important. Deciding what percentage of your portfolio should be put into stocks, mutual funds or bonds isn't simple, particularly for those reaching retirement age. Imagine saving for 30 or more years only to see the stock market decline in the years before your retirement! For many, this is what happened during the bear market of 2000 through 2002. To determine your asset allocation plan, we strongly suggest you speak to a financial advisor who can customize a plan that is right for you.

In general, the key to asset allocation is investing in assets with dissimilar performance. This is true because when investing in assets with similar behavior, whichever direction an investment takes, the others follow. With proper asset allocation, the upward movement of one asset will offset some part of the downward movement of another.

While the scientific and measurable investment principles of asset allocation are sound and are well proven, up until recently the process required some detailed mathematical calculations. After all, it involves examining the world of investments, analyzing performance, calculating risk, and then artfully combining those investments in proper proportions to achieve the individual investor's plan objectives within pre-determined levels of investment risk. It is so complicated, in fact, that two of its modern theoretical fathers, Harry Markowitz and William Sharpe, shared a Nobel Prize for their groundbreaking efforts in developing this model.

Modern Portfolio Theory

Modern Portfolio Theory (MPT) is the philosophical opposite of traditional stock picking. It is the creation of economists, who try to understand the market as a whole, rather than business analysts, who look for what makes each investment opportunity unique. Investments are described statistically, in terms of their expected long-term return rate and their expected short-term volatility. The volatility is equated with "risk", measuring how much worse than average an investment's bad years are likely to be. The goal is to identify your acceptable level of risk tolerance, and then to find a portfolio with the maximum expected return for that level of risk.

Actually MPT is the theory on how risk-averse investors can construct portfolios in order to optimize market risk against expected returns. The theory emphasizes that risk should not be viewed in a negative context, but rather as an inherent part of higher reward. According to the theory, an efficient frontier of optimal portfolios can be constructed offering the maximum possible expected return for a given level of risk.

It is also called "portfolio theory," "portfolio management theory" or "Markowitz Portfolio Theory"; Harry Markowitz pioneered it in his paper "Portfolio Selection," published in 1952 by the Journal of Finance. Thirty-eight years later, he shared a Nobel Prize with Merton Miller and William Sharpe for what has become a broad theory for portfolio selection.

Markowitz Portfolio Theory provides a broad context for understanding the interactions of systematic risk and reward. It has profoundly shaped how institutional portfolios are managed, and motivated the use of passive investment management techniques. The mathematics of portfolio theory is used extensively in financial risk management and was a theoretical precursor for today's value-at-risk measures.

There are 4 basic steps:

-Security Valuation
-Asset Allocation
-Portfolio Optimization
-Performance Measurement

Random Walk Theory

Random walk theory gained popularity in 1973 when Burton Malkiel wrote "A Random Walk Down Wall Street", a book that is now regarded as an investment classic. Random walk is a stock market theory that states that the past movement or direction of the price of a stock or overall market cannot be used to predict its future movement. Originally examined by Maurice Kendall in 1953, the theory states that stock price fluctuations are independent of each other and have the same probability distribution, but, over a period of time, prices maintain an upward trend.

In short, random walk says that stocks take a random and unpredictable path. The chance of a stock's future price going up is the same as it going down. A follower of random walk believes it is impossible to outperform the market without assuming additional risk. In his book, Malkiel preaches that both technical analysis and fundamental analysis are largely a waste of time and are still unproven in outperforming the markets.

Malkiel constantly states that a long-term buy-and-hold strategy is the best and that individuals should not attempt to time the markets. Attempts based on technical, fundamental, or any other analysis is futile. He backs this up with statistics showing that most mutual funds fail to beat benchmark averages like the S&P 500.

While many still follow the preaching of Malkiel, others believe that the investing landscape is very different than it was when Malkiel wrote his book, nearly 30 years ago. Today, everyone has easy and fast access to relevant news and stock quotes. Investing is no longer a game for the privileged. Random walk has never been a popular concept with those on Wall Street, probably because it condemns analysis and stock picking, the foundation of Wall Street.

How much truth is there in this theory? It's tough to say. There is evidence that supports both sides of the debate. Our suggestion is to pick up a copy of Malkiel's book and draw your own conclusions.

The Efficient Frontier

Suppose you have data for a collection of securities (like the S & P 500 stocks, for example), and you graph the return rates and standard deviations for these securities, and for all portfolios you can get by allocating among them. Markowitz showed that you get a region bounded by an upward-sloping curve, which he called the efficient frontier.

It's clear that for any given value of standard deviation, you would like to choose a portfolio that gives you the greatest possible rate of return; so you always want a portfolio that lies up along the efficient frontier, rather than lower down, in the interior of the region. This is the first important property of the efficient frontier: it's where the best portfolios are.

The second important property of the efficient frontier is that it's curved, not straight. This is actually significant—in fact, it's the key to how diversification lets you improve your reward-to-risk ratio. To see why, imagine a 50/50 allocation between just two securities. Assuming that the year-to-year performance of these two securities is not perfectly in sync—that is, assuming that the great years and the lousy years for Security 1 don't correspond perfectly to the great years and lousy years for Security 2, but that their cycles are at least a little off—then the standard deviation of the 50/50 allocation will be less than the average of the standard deviations of the two securities separately. Graphically, this stretches the possible allocations to the left of the straight line joining the two securities.

In statistical terms, this effect is due to lack of covariance. The smaller the covariance between the two securities—the more out of sync they are—the smaller the standard deviation of a portfolio that combines them. The ultimate would be to find two securities with negative covariance (very out of sync: the best years of one happen during the worst years of the other, and vice versa).

The Optimal Portfolio

This concept of the modern portfolio falls under the "modern portfolio theory." The theory also assumes (among other things) that investors fanatically try to minimize risk while striving for the highest return possible. The theory states that investors will act rationally, always making decisions aimed at maximizing their return for their acceptable level of risk.

Harry Markowitz used the optimal portfolio in 1952, and it shows us that it is possible for different portfolios to have varying levels of risk and return. Each investor must decide how much risk they can handle and than allocate (or diversify) their portfolio according to this decision.

The chart below is a graphical example of how the optimal portfolio works. The optimal-risk portfolio is usually determined to be somewhere in the middle of the curve because, as you go higher up the curve, you take on proportionately more risk for a lower incremental return. On the other end, low risk/low return portfolios are pointless because you can achieve a similar return by investing in risk-free assets, like government securities.

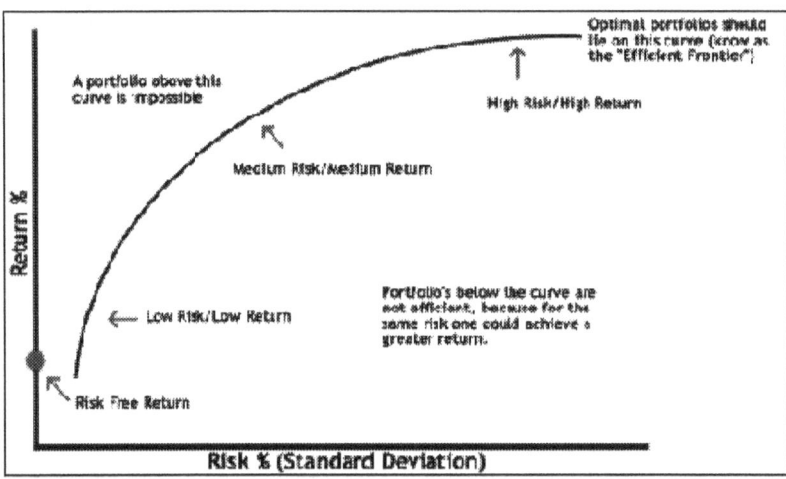

You can choose how much volatility you are willing to bear in your portfolio by picking any other point that falls on the "efficient frontier." This will give you the maximum return for the amount of risk you wish to accept. Optimizing your portfolio is not something you can calculate in your head. There are computer programs that are dedicated to determining optimal portfolios by estimating hundreds (and sometimes thousands) of different expected returns for each given amount of risk.

Efficient Market Hypothesis

Efficient Market Hypothesis (EMH) is an idea partly developed in the 1960s by Eugene Fama. It states that it is impossible to beat the market because prices already incorporate and reflect all relevant information. This is also a highly controversial and often disputed theory. Supporters of this model believe it is pointless to search for undervalued stocks or try to predict trends in the market through any technique (fundamental or technical analysis).

Under the efficient market hypothesis, any time you buy and sell securities, you're engaging in a game of chance, not skill. If markets are efficient and current, it means that prices always reflect all information, so there are no way you'll ever be able to buy a stock at a bargain price.

This theory has been met with a lot of opposition, especially from the technical analysts. Their argument against the efficient market theory is that many investors base their expectations on past prices, past earnings, track records, and other indicators. Since stock prices are largely based on investor expectation, many believe it only makes sense to believe that past prices do influence future prices.

PART II

Retirement Planning

"Making Sure Your Money Lasts As Long As You Do"

The Dangers of Inflation

Even though the United States economy continues to grow and prosper it still faces the reality of inflation. Inflation can be described as a decrease in the value of the dollar, which causes prices to rise.

Inflation can be caused by several different factors. Inflation can be a direct result of goods and services being in great demand and the economy not being able to satisfy this demand; this is called *down-pull inflation*. Another cause of inflation is when the cost of doing business is increased which is called *cost-push inflation*. When the Federal Reserve raises interest rates, financial markets increase their prices.

People who depend on fixed incomes are hurt by inflation because their income loses its value.

This said, one of the biggest problems in planning retirement finances is price inflation—the continuous increases in the cost-of-living over the years. Many wonder how financial planning is possible when future costs and income levels seem so unpredictable. Even relatively low rates of inflation can cause prices to more than double in the 15-20 years most of us can expect to be retired.

For example, if the annual inflation rate is 4%, the purchasing power of your income is reduced by 50% in 16 years. In 30 years, the purchasing power of that income is reduced by 75%.

Fifty dollars today doesn't buy what it used to ten years ago; how much less will your money be worth ten years from now? One widely used measurement for projecting inflation rates is the Consumer Price Index (CPI).The CPI is the representative cost of a "basket of goods". The actual price of the basket of goods is not that important. What is critical is the amount of change, specifically the 12 month change, stated as a percentage. This percentage change is known as the rate of inflation.

To plan an adequate income stream for your retirement, we should apply the expected annual CPI to your planned retirement income. This will determine just how much buying power your retirement income will have. This works as follows:

- First, estimate how much annual income you will need to live the lifestyle you want, in today's currency.

- Second, multiply this amount by one plus the annual rate of inflation. For example, if you think you will need $20,000 a year and the expected annual rate of inflation is 5%:

  $20,000 x (1 + 0.05) = 21,000$

- You will actually need $21,000 to cover your expenses after a year— inclusive of the cost of rising inflation.

Repeat the calculation, using your new total, for every year you plan to wait before drawing on your savings at retirement. The results may surprise you. For example, the effects of 10 years of inflation means you will need $25,525 (approx) to meet those same expenses. Thus, you need to consider the effect of inflation on your expected retirement income when planning for retirement.

How Inflation Affects Retirement Income

As we've already stressed financial planning should result in maintaining or improving the purchasing power of your money. Being able to retire with the assurance of adequate purchasing power for the next 10, 20 or 30 years is important.

Here are some typical sources of retirement income and a description of how they are affected by inflation:

Social Security: By law, Social Security benefits are tied to increases in the Consumer Price Index (CPI). If a person's Social Security benefit is $850 a month at the time of retirement, that amount will be adjusted each year with full cost-of-living adjustments (COLAs). In other words, the purchasing power of the benefit remains exactly the same from the very first check to the very last.

Pension Plans: The majority of pension plans provide a fixed payment, which is the same amount of money each month for the life of the person. But some employers agree to increase pension amounts as the cost-of-living rises—either through periodic adjustments (requiring legislative action each time) or automatic annual cost-of-living adjustments. Even the latter, however, are almost never full cost-of-living adjustments. They are generally capped at a certain percentage (commonly 3%); regardless of how high inflation may rise in a year.

Fixed Annuities: Annuities guarantee a fixed income for a specified period, such as 10 years or life. A person may purchase an annuity that pays $200 a month for life beginning at age 62. If the person lives until age 92, the $200 would be paid monthly for the entire period. There would be no adjustment for changes in the cost-of-living over the 30 years.

Savings Accounts and Investments: Savings accounts tend to pay a fixed-percentage rate of interest. Keep in mind that if the annual rate of return (the yield) is less than the inflation rate, the purchasing power of these savings and investments will be eroded over time. Stocks and commodities often deliver the highest rates of return in the long term. As a result, these types of investments may turn out to be a good hedge against inflation. But they also carry higher risks, which must be recognized by any potential investor and weighed against potential returns.

The Need for Growth

We all know, after spending years working hard, setting up your home and raising a family, retirement should be one of the most rewarding chapters of your life. Whereas, it should be the time to enjoy your independence, sometimes the situation becomes very pathetic in the lack of proper planning. We all wish to spend time with children and grandchildren, traveling, pursuing a hobby, embarking on a new vocation and doing those things that we were not able to do when we were young and committed to our jobs.

However, for too many people, the insecurity of their retirement income clouds this sunny picture. Even though you have planned ahead and saved, will your money be enough to last for a lifetime? Is there some way your savings could provide a constant source of income that would ensure peace of mind? These are some of the most important questions, which need to be addressed well before retirement.

Today, thanks to a healthier life style and advances in medicine, the average person lives longer. A person, who is 60 plus today, can hope to live at least till the age of 75. A person who is 40 plus today can hope to live at least till the age of 80. That means that we need to plan for at least 20 to 30 years of retired life. Each of us probably has a blurred idea of how we want to live in retirement. Few people, though, have given much thought to what a satisfying retirement life style might really cost.

You might be pleasantly surprised to learn that you can afford to continue your present life style, or you may find that only by taking decisive action now will you be able to achieve a satisfying, secure way of life in retirement. None of us can afford to leave our future well being to chance. Even if your employer has a most generous pension plan, you should determine if your income from all possible sources will provide the income you most likely will need when you retire.

Here's an important point:

Your future income needs will depend partly on how you desire to live, what is acceptable to you, and what is realistically achievable.

Below are two methods for estimating your retirement income target. If you are married, you and your spouse will need to figure your expected income needs both as a couple and as individual survivors.

Method One: The Annual Expense Method

Using the annual expense method, a person or couple estimates what typical monthly and annual expenses will be in retirement. In making this estimate, look at what you are currently spending; estimate how this will change in retirement, and create a "retirement budget."

The form given below is helpful in using this method. Note that the form asks you to first estimate your current monthly and periodic expenses. Next, you are asked to estimate what your monthly and periodic expenses will be when you retire. If you are expecting to retire with a spouse, a relative, friend, etc., be sure to include his or her expenses as well as your own.

Worksheet: Annual Expense Method

Regular Expenses	Current Monthly Expenses	Estimated Monthly Expenses*
Mortgage or rent		
Utilities, telephone		
Groceries		
Work expenses (commuting, lunches, etc.)		
Entertainment, eating out		
Recreation (e.g. golf)		
Clothes		
Laundry, cleaning		
Personal (barber, beauty salon)		
Auto operation, transportation		
Education (adult courses)		
Education of children (e.g. college expenses)		
Donations		
Support of others (e.g., alimony)		
Loans (auto, other)		
Regular services (e.g., lawn service)		
Miscellaneous expenses		
Total Regular Expenses		
PERIODIC EXPENSES	*Current Expenses (Average per month)*	*Estimated Retirement Expenses (Average per month)*
Real estate taxes		
Household maintenance		
New household purchases		
Casualty insurance (auto, home)		
Life insurance		
Disability, medical insurance		
Vacations		
Gifts (birthdays, anniversaries, Christmas)		
Income taxes (local, state, federal)		
Legal services		
Medical, dental, veterinarian		
SAVINGS AND INVESTMENTS		
Life insurance		
Real estate		
Securities		
Miscellaneous		
Total periodic expenses		
Total monthly expenses		
Total annual expenses		

Estimated Annual Income Needed As a Couple $_____

Estimated Annual Income Needed (Survivor #1) $_____

Estimated Annual Income Needed (Survivor #2) $_____

Note: *Assume prices will be the same as they are today. Adjustments for inflation can be done later.

Method Two: The Three—Fourths Rule

Some experts suggest that monthly retirement income needs to be about ¾ (three-fourths) of pre-retirement income in order to adequately meet all of your future expenses. This means that if your income in the year before you retire is $20,000, you should consider planning a retirement income that adds up to $15,000 a year. Judgment must be exercised in using this method. Individuals with relatively low incomes may need more than three-fourths of their pre-retirement income to meet retirement expenses. Similarly, a couple with a high pre-retirement income might need less than three-fourths of that amount as their retirement income.

As with the first method, if you are expecting to retire with a spouse, relative, friend, etc., be sure to include his or her income if it will be used to meet your household expenses.

A surviving spouse will probably require a retirement income that is three-fourths of what the couple together required. For example, if the couple required $1,600 per month as retirement income, a surviving spouse might require $1,200 per month. Since the actual amount needed will vary with specific people and circumstances, consider your own case carefully when planning for your future.

Worksheet: Currently Expected Retirement Income

"Currently expected retirement income" refers to the income you can expect to receive from Social Security, Pension Plans and any other arrangement you have made for regular retirement income. From your list of financial assets, determine the sources and amounts of your currently expected retirement income. Generally, this information will include pensions, Social Security if you are eligible and annuities.

Now list your currently expected monthly retirement income.

Couples, or any two people retiring together, need to compute what each would receive if he or she were the survivor. For example, the survivor #1 column below could list what the husband would receive if his wife dies, and the survivor #2 columns could list what the wife would receive if her husband dies.

	ESTIMATED MONTHLY AMOUNT		
Type Or Source	Individual Or Couple	Survivor #1	Survivor #2

Fears of Retirement

Recognize that your fears of retirement are really fears of change—which may not be bad—and get to them before they get to you. Giving up your career identity can be very scary. It's a lot like giving up smoking—but you'll feel so much better in the end.

—Peter Greeman, Former Advertising Executive

Outliving My Money

In the past 20 years the population of the United States grew by 200 million people, reaching 850 million people in the year 2000. The annual rate of growth varies from 1.3% for the general population to 1.7% for the urban population, to more than 2% for the population over 65 years and to rates between 3% and 5% for those over 85 years-old, the fastest-growing group. Medical science has presented you the retiree with a brand new concern. Outliving your income!

Nursing care, whether received in your home, an assisted living facility, or a nursing home, is expensive. The cost of nursing home care may be close to $10,000 per month or more in certain regions of the United States. Although you may never need nursing care, the fact is that almost half of the population will one day face these costs.

The number one "fear of retirement" is one outliving one's money. In today's high-tech world, people are living longer, healthier lives. We often see a popular bumper sticker which reads, "I'm spending my children's' inheritance!" The danger in this is, when you're done with this process, you may get some discouraging news from your doctor, you've got twenty years to Live!"

Don't make the mistake many other retirees have made. Work with a qualified financial advisor to make sure that your investment portfolio is properly diversified and balanced. *Remember, your investment portfolio has to grow greater than the inflation rate **after** you take out your income!*

In retirement planning, a question often asked is "How long will my money last?" The following chart may help in figuring how long your money will last if you start drawing it out.

How Long Will Your Money Last?					
This chart shows how long your money will last if you withdraw a fixed amount each year.					
% of capital	Years money will last if invested and withdrawn at these rates:				
	5%	6%	7%	8%	9%	10%
8%	21	24	31	*	*	*
10%	15	16	18	21	27	*
12%	11	12	13	15	17	19
14%	10	10	11	12	12	14
16%	8	9	9	10	10	11
18%	7	7	8	8	9	9
20%	6	7	7	7	7	8

An * means it will last indefinitely at that rate.

Catastrophic Illness

Severe illness requiring prolonged hospitalization or recovery; usually involves high costs for hospitals and doctors and medicines. The greatest threat facing older people and their families today may be the financial, social, psychological and familial consequences of needing long-term care.

Long-Term Care Planning

To understand long-term geriatric care you must first understand the difference between skilled and custodial care.

Skilled care is anything that requires a licensed professional to provide. It can be very difficult criteria to meet. Many people believe that personal care is a nursing service, but this is not the case. Nurses are skilled medical professionals and their services are used for the more clinical aspects such as wound care, post-surgical follow-up or monitoring health status.

Custodial care is assistance with Activities of Daily Living (ADLs). That is: eating, bathing, dressing, continence, mobility and transferring.

Most people receiving long-term care require just custodial care. And, since Medicare does not cover any of the cost associated with custodial care, the individual or family pays for the total expense. This can be very costly. This is why considering long-term care insurance is such an important part of your future planning.

Consider the following:[2]

- ➢ Over 50% of all people over 65 need "custodial" care at home, in an adult day care center, in a residential facility or nursing home. For every 1000 people…

    - o   5 will have a House Fire (the average loss is $3,428)

    - o   70 will have an Auto Accident (the average loss is $3,000)

    - o   600 will need Long Term Care (The average cost is $40,000 to $80,000 per year)

- ➢ You are prepared for just about everything—except the coverage you're most likely to need—Long Term Care Insurance.

- ➢ Contrary to common belief Medicare, Supplements, health insurance & HMO's don't cover long term "custodial" care at all. Only "skilled" care is covered for very limited periods of time. To qualify for Medicaid, you must "spend down" most of your lifetime savings. Also, a new Federal law levies "criminal penalties" for certain asset transfers designed to create or hasten Medicaid eligibility.

---

[2] Source: Society of American Actuaries, 1995 & HIAA, 1994

> ➤ How much will long term care cost? Now it costs $40,000 to $80,000 a year or more for possibly many years—totaling hundreds of thousands of dollars! What will long term care cost in the future? Who will pay for long-term care? Long Term Care Insurance could be the answer. "The Health Insurance Portability and Accountability Act of 1996" gives tax advantages for the purchase of long term care insurance.

Long-Term Care Insurance

Long-Term Care Insurance can help you:

- Protect your family from the catastrophic costs of long term care;

- Remain in control of your assets; and,

- Maintain your own independence and dignity.

Private long-term care insurance is a way to avoid spending all of your assets when long-term care is needed. Long term care in a New York Metropolitan Area nursing home costs about $71,000 per year (more in the New York City area). The cost of long-term care insurance depends on your age, the benefits you choose, the length of coverage and other factors.

Long-term care insurance policies vary widely in the coverage they provide, and consumers are wise to do some research before purchasing any long-term care insurance policy. As you or other members of your family enter your 50's, 60's, 70's and beyond, part of retirement planning should include long term care. Will your parents or loved one's need long term care?

Who Should Consider Long-Term Care Insurance?

Anyone who is over 50 and who wants to ensure they stay in control of where they receive care and who provides that care, should consider long-term care insurance. Even if you don't have thousands of dollars in savings to protect, you should consider a home care only policy, so you can receive care at home for as long as possible.

When you buy at a younger age, you have a better chance at receiving a preferred health discount and can consider a lifetime benefit. When you are younger, there are more things that could happen to spur the need for long-term care for a short time; for example, a year of rehabilitation after a stroke, chemotherapy treatment, or surgery that requires a period of rehabilitation.

Yes, you would be paying longer but the lower premiums when you buy young still make it less expensive overall than waiting.

"LTC insurance" can also work like a long-term disability policy. While disability insurance is intended for income replacement, it is not intended to provide for the custodial care that is necessary when illness unexpectedly strikes.

Employer Sponsored Plans Distribution

General Rules[3]

1. Normal distributions are taxed at your then current income tax rate. All earnings and pretax contributions are subject to taxation.

2. Distributions can begin without penalty after age 59 ½.

3. Distributions made prior to age 59 ½ are subject to a 10% penalty on top of regular income taxes if they do not qualify for one of the following exceptions:

- Death.

- Disability (as defined by the IRS).

- If withdrawal is distributed as "substantially equal payments."

- If you leave your job for any reason and are between ages 55 and 59 ½.

- Payments for deductible medical expenses.

4. Early lump-sum distributions can result in substantial tax obligations.

5. Rollovers, both direct and indirect, to other qualified plans and traditional IRAs preserve tax deferral.

6. Indirect rollovers are subject to a mandatory tax withholding of 20% of the taxable portion. The remaining 80% must be rolled over within 60 days to a new retirement account or else it is subject to the 10% tax mentioned above in addition to regular income taxes. (You may want to add the 20% into your rollover from your own pocket to avoid having it taxed and penalized as a distribution.)

---

[3] Retirement Planning Series, Standard & Poor's

7. Generally, distributions must begin no later than April 1 following the year in which you turn 70 ½. Some plans allow you to delay taking distributions if you continue working beyond age 70 ½.

8. Following your first distribution, each subsequent withdrawal must occur before December 31 of each year. If you fail to take the money out in a timely manner, or if you take out less than required, you'll be subject to a 50% penalty tax on the difference between what should have been withdrawn and the actual withdrawal amount.

Annuitization vs. IRA Rollover

Annuitization

"Annuitize" is a word you may not be familiar with unless you work for an insurance company. This term is not even found in some dictionaries. A fairly simple definition of "Annuitize" would be, "To receive regular payments at regular time intervals for a lifetime or for a specific period of time."

You can tailor the income you receive from your Annuity, be it variable or fixed, to match your needs, including the option to provide you with a steady stream of income that you can't outlive.[4]

If you are a variable annuity owner, then you are already taking advantage of one of its great benefits—the ability to accumulate wealth for your future while deferring all taxes until money is actually withdrawn from your account. The time will come, however, when you need to start living off your retirement savings and other sources of income, such as Social Security. That's the time when another important and unique feature of your annuity can play a critical role—the ability to "annuitize" the money you have saved over the years.

One of the real attractions of an annuity contract at retirement is that you can receive a stream of income that will be guaranteed for life. Therefore, you can never outlive your income. It helps you to overcome one of the hazards of living beyond your expectations. You can also choose to receive payments for a set period of time, such as 10 or 20 years.

---

[4] Payment is based on the claims-paying ability of the insurer. Prospectuses for the products and any underlying funds, which contain more complete information, including all charges and expenses, should be consulted first which may be available from your financial advisor.

You can receive payments that:

- Will last as long as you live (a "life annuity")

- Will last as long both you and your spouse (or other person you select) live (a "joint and survivor annuity")

- Will last for your lifetime and/or a specific period of time (a "life with period certain annuity")

- Will last for a specific period of time (a "period certain annuity")

- Will pay a specified amount of money per month until your account is depleted (a "fixed amount annuity")

When choosing to annuitize, you can also decide whether your payments will be fixed or variable:

- With the fixed option, you'll receive the same amount each period (on a monthly, quarterly, semi-annual, or annual basis).

- With the variable option, the amount of your payments will vary depending on the investment performance of the options you have selected.

The maximum age at which you can annuitize is 95 (Some qualified plans may require annuitization at an earlier age.) It is important to keep in mind that you cannot change your annuitization payment choice once payments have started. So be sure to consult your financial or tax advisor before selecting a payment option.

IRA

Certainly, one of the main benefits of an IRA is that earnings on contributions accumulate on a tax-deferred basis. Over the long term, this can potentially generate significant additional savings. At the same time, Internal Revenue Service (IRS) withdrawal rules are generally geared toward ensuring that the benefits of IRA growth are not carried forward into future generations. Therefore, your death could trigger mandatory withdrawals from your IRA, resulting in a loss of the ability to maintain the IRA's benefit of long-term, tax-deferred growth.

With their tax-advantages[5], IRAs have always been an excellent way to save for retirement. As of 2002, you can save even more for your retirement as the maximum annual contribution limit for IRAs ($2,000 in 2001) has been increased substantially. New tax law also enables individuals age 50 or over to make "catch up" contributions of $500 each year for tax years 2002 through 2005. An additional $1,000 catch up contribution can be made in 2006 and thereafter.

Contribution Limits		
Tax Year	Standard IRA Limit*	Those Aged 50 and Over
2002	$3,000	$3,500
2003	$3,000	$3,500
2004	$3,000	$3,500
2005	$4,000	$4,500
2006	$4,000	$5,000
2007	$4,000	$5,000
2008	$5,000	$6,000

*For tax years beginning in 2008 and thereafter, the $5,000 limit will be adjusted for inflation in $500 increments.

Your Options Include:

Traditional IRA

In a traditional IRA, earnings grow tax-deferred. That means earnings (and deductible contributions) are taxed upon withdrawal. However, with a traditional IRA, annual contributions—and catch-up contributions, if you qualify—may be tax-deductible. (See the contribution limit chart above.) Any working taxpayer under 70 1/2 can contribute to a traditional IRA.

---

[5] Distributions subject to tax. Distributions prior to age 59 1/2 are subject to an additional 10% tax penalty.

Roth IRA

In a Roth IRA, earnings grow tax-free and there are no taxes when those earnings are withdrawn (subject to certain restrictions)[6]. While you can withdraw contributions at anytime without being penalized or taxed, contributions are not deductible on your tax returns. While there is no age limit to contribute to a Roth IRA, you must meet certain modified adjusted gross income requirements.

Who is eligible?

Generally, you can contribute to a Roth IRA if you have taxable compensation and your modified adjusted gross income is less than:

- $160,000 for married individuals filing jointly,

- $110,000 for single or head of household, and

- $10,000 for individuals who are married but filing separate returns

SEP IRA

The Simplified Employee Pension (SEP) IRA is ideal for small business owners like doctors, independent contractors, freelancers, or those with a family business. Annual contribution limits (as of this writing) are 20% of total net compensation or up to $40,000 per year. Contributions are tax-deductible, earnings grow tax deferred, and it is relatively simple to administer.

Simple IRA

A Savings Incentive Match Plan for Employees (SIMPLE) IRA is a tax-deferred retirement plan offered by sole proprietors or businesses with less than 100 employees who do not maintain or contribute to any other retirement plan. The maximum annual employee contribution (as of this writing) is $7,000. In addition, employer contributions must be either a 100% match for all employees (up to 3% of your total compensation), or 2% for all eligible employees (to a maximum of $3,200)

---

6 · Contributions can be withdrawn at any time with no taxes or penalties.
- · Earnings can be withdrawn with no penalties or taxes if the account is 5 years old and the holder is 59 1/2; for disability or death; for certain home purchases.
- · If earnings are withdrawn before account is 5 years old or the holder is 59 1/2, earnings are subject to 10% penalty and taxes.

IRA rollover

Money that has already accumulated in a workplace retirement plan or another IRA can still be protected from current taxation by utilizing an IRA rollover. The use of a rollover is most common when an individual leaves an employer, but wishes to keep the retirement plan money intact in a tax-deferred account. When handled correctly, a rollover will maintain the tax-deferred integrity of your retirement plan.

Basic Rules Regarding Rollovers

If you are moving money from an employer's plan or another IRA to a rollover IRA, here are some basic rules that apply:

- Once the money is paid out of the old plan, and paid to you directly, you have 60 days to move the full amount to the IRA to avoid taxes and withdrawal penalties (if applicable).

- A 20% automatic tax withholding applies to the rollover if the payout from the old plan goes directly to you before you roll the money into the new IRA. Therefore, make sure the rollover goes directly from the custodian of your old plan to your IRA custodian. When handled in that way, the automatic withholding provision does not apply.

- If you think you might want to eventually move the money in the rollover IRA to another employer's plan, be sure to keep it separate from other IRA dollars. Establish this "conduit IRA" as its own account.

- Be sure only pre-tax contributions from a workplace retirement plan are moved into the IRA. Any assets attributable to after-tax contributions at work must be invested separately.

Why It Is Always Better To Rollover

For many people who are changing jobs or approaching retirement, an IRA rollover is the most feasible option, as there are several benefits as compared to staying with your 401(k) or opting for annuitization. For example, the money from your old plan will continue to compound tax-deferred and you will be most likely to have access to more investment options, as well as the ability to adjust your investment strategy as you see fit. Furthermore, you can take distributions if and when you like, subject to IRS regulations.

I have worked with many people who initially found rolling-over a bit daunting due to lack of knowledge and experience. However, after working with my team and setting up an IRA rollover account, they came to realize that it was the best financial decision they had ever made. A rollover is merely a transfer of 401(k) plan assets from your 401(k) to your IRA. It paves the way for you to take advantage of powerful tax and investment options generally not available within your 401(k) plan.

Regardless of how well your 401(k) may be performing, the rollover IRA option should be selected because it will allow most retirees to accumulate and pass on more money to their children or other loved ones.

The problem, however, is that many people leave their retirement dollars with their 401(k)s, and their families do not gain the IRA benefits. You don't have to leave your money with your company just because you worked there. I've come to realize that many retirees have a false sense of loyalty to the company that employed them for so many years. Loyalty is a good thing and in short supply these days, but when it comes to your retirement savings, your first loyalty must be to yourself and your loved ones.

Upon retirement, or even changing jobs, you should generally roll your company retirement plan money to an IRA to take advantage of the estate planning and tax options available. The same holds true for self-employed people with "Keogh" accounts. That money should be rolled to an IRA.

The first thing many former employees will say when they are advised to roll the money to an IRA is that the company plan account is doing so well and "I don't want to touch it." That's a poor reason. If you rolled over to an IRA you could have the identical investments in your IRA and work with a financial advisor rather than being forced to default to the limited company investment options. In your own IRA, you have the widest possible range of investment choices and can tailor those options to your specific situation. Moreover, you'll also find that once you leave your company, any questions about your account must go through some "human resources" department, which rarely has any human qualities. In fact, you're usually looped into some computer phone recording maze and do not receive the personal attention you and your retirement savings deserve.

Stretch Your IRA

The biggest benefit to rolling over your company plan money to your IRA is the estate planning that can be accomplished by taking advantage what is commonly know as a "Stretch IRA."

The "Stretch IRA" is the ability for your retirement money to outlive you and be stretched over the life of your IRA beneficiary, who may be much younger than you. The IRS allows a younger beneficiary (a child, for example) to stretch distributions of the inherited IRA over his or her longer life expectancy, resulting in possibly decades of further tax-deferred growth on the account. The way to make the most of your IRA is to keep it growing tax deferred over the longest possible period.

This option is generally not available in a company plan because the company can make their own policy regarding your retirement tax options. Moreover, it is not the company's obligation to provide an estate plan for you and your family. They also don't want the administrative responsibility. In fact, they wish you would take your money and leave and stop bothering them. You see, you're only an ex-employee now.

Although the IRS allows this "Stretch-Out", most company plans do not, and will force a full payout or a payout over some limited term, such as five years. So, if your child is the beneficiary of your 401(k), when you die, the company will usually pay out the entire IRA to your child, triggering a fully taxable distribution and ending any further tax deferral. Let's take a closer look at this essential planning tool.

The Stretch IRA Strategy

The "Stretch IRA" Strategy is a wealth-transfer strategy that allows you to extend the period of tax-deferred earnings on the assets of a pre-existing, or newly established, IRA by passing your IRA assets to a younger beneficiary. Under IRS regulations issued in 2002, any individual who holds a traditional IRA can change the beneficiary to "stretch" IRA distributions. If you do not need to live on your IRA assets and want to benefit younger generations, consider using the Stretch IRA strategy.

In another words, the Stretch IRA is a strategy designed to maximize your IRA's tax deferral during your lifetime and help leave a legacy for your heirs. However, the Stretch IRA may not be suitable for every investor. It is typically designed for account owners whose goal is to leave assets to their heirs and have other sources of income other than their IRA to fund their retirement expenses. By working with your financial advisor, you can determine if the stretch strategy makes sense for you.

How Does It Work?

In general:

- For your newly established or existing IRA, you name either your spouse or younger individuals (e.g., your children or grandchildren) as primary beneficiaries.

- During your lifetime, after you attain age 70½, your required minimum distributions are usually based on the joint and last survivor life expectancy of you and a beneficiary assumed to be 10 years younger. However, if your sole beneficiary is your spouse who is more than 10 years younger than you, distributions will be based on your and your spouse's actual joint and last survivor life expectancy.

- After your death, if you have named your spouse and he or she survives you, your spouse may roll over the remaining assets to his or her own IRA and name younger individuals (e.g., children or grandchildren) as beneficiaries.

- The required minimum distributions will then be based on the joint life and last survivor expectancy of the surviving spouse and a 10-year-younger beneficiary.

- After your spouse's death, or following your death if you named a younger individual directly, the younger individual may receive the required minimum distributions based on his or her remaining life expectancy.

- Distributions to the beneficiary will continue until the IRA is depleted.

- To ensure the success of the Stretch IRA strategy, make sure your beneficiaries understand their part in extending the life of an inherited IRA, as beneficiaries may withdraw the entire remaining balance of an IRA.

Benefits of a Stretch IRA

Provides tax-efficient wealth transfer:

- The law requires that once you reach age 70½, you must withdraw a required amount from your traditional IRA each year. When you choose to withdraw no more than those required distributions from your IRA and designate a younger beneficiary, you can extend the life of your IRA.

- Under the new IRS regulations, if you have an individual designated beneficiary, your beneficiary will not be required to completely withdraw your IRA assets either within five years of your death or over your remaining life expectancy. When a younger beneficiary inherits an IRA, the remaining balance can be paid out over the younger person's single life expectancy, effectively stretching out the length of time that withdrawals can be taken from that IRA. This extends the period of tax-deferred earnings of assets within an IRA beyond the lifetime of the person who set up the IRA.

- Payments to beneficiaries are paid out as death distributions, which are not subject to the 10% penalty tax even for a beneficiary under age 59½.

Retain control of the IRA:

- Most of the Stretch IRA planning is revocable. So, for example, if your financial situation changes and you need more income in retirement, you can take larger IRA distributions as needed. However, once you reach age 70½, you can't request a smaller amount than your required minimum distributions.

- Similarly, if the beneficiary's situation changes after the death of the owner, he or she can, usually, take distributions exceeding the required minimum distributions.

- You can change your beneficiary at any time. In most cases, such a change would not affect the amount of required minimum distributions during your lifetime.

Naming and Distribution of Beneficiaries

Choosing your beneficiaries is an essential step for implementing your stretch strategy. If the IRA is not set up properly, your beneficiary will reduce his or her likelihood of extending the IRA's tax-deferred growth as far into the future as possible. Even worse, they could be faced with is a significant tax burden. There are a number of options when it comes to choosing your IRA beneficiaries.

Your choices include individuals (relatives or non-relatives) or entities such as charities, universities, a trust or your estate.

The remaining balance can be paid out to the beneficiary over his or her designated lifetime, after the IRA owner dies, by using his or her life expectancy and not the account owner's. Moreover, it is also important for the account owner to name contingent beneficiates as well. In the situations when the designated beneficiary should disclaim their interest from the inherited IRA, they can name the contingent beneficiary as the designated beneficiary, as long as it is within 9 months. By simply naming a beneficiary, or a contingent beneficiary, the IRA holder gains the maximum stretch out of the IRA assets after his or her death.

Consolidate Retirement Assets and Establish Separate Accounts

One of the most striking part of IRAs is that it offers choices and flexibility that you will not find in such employer-sponsored plans like 401(k)s. Consider rolling your assets from any former employer plans into your IRA. Then bring all of your IRAs under one roof with the help of your financial advisor, making it easier to put an overall stretch IRA strategy into place.

Multiple beneficiaries of an inherited IRA have until December 31 of the year after the account owner dies to split the inherited IRA into individual accounts and use their own life expectancies to calculate the remaining distributions. If the IRA is not split into separate accounts at that time, then the Required Minimum Distribution ("RMD") of the account would be calculated using the oldest beneficiary's life expectancy. In the following example, the IRA owner named three beneficiaries. By splitting a $500,000 IRA into three separate IRAs, the beneficiaries stretched the IRA to over $4 million in distributions.[7]

Inherited Ira Assets	Beneficiary	Life expectancy used for calculations	Distributions
$250,000	Spouse age 70[7]	17	$683,986
$125,000	Child, age 40	43.6	$1,067,574
$125,000	Child, age 35	48.5	$1,416,103
		Total	$3,167,663

---

[7] A spouse beneficiary also has the option of treating an inherited IRA as his/her own. In this case, the spouse beneficiary would roll the assets over to an Ira in his or her own name and take distributions using the Uniform Lifetime table, based on his/her own life expectancy, recalculated. She/he can then name his/her own beneficiary for the account, potentially stretching the IRA assets even further.

Review Account Titling

It is essential that your accounts are titled properly. It's important that your name as IRA owner stay in the account registration. The wrong registration could mean forfeiting the account's ability to stretch.

It makes sense to sit down with your financial advisor at least annually to go over your beneficiary designations. Your situation could change and you might want to designate new beneficiaries. Was there a divorce or death in the family or possibly an addition such a child and grandchild? With the help of your financial advisor, you can continue to implement the stretch strategy for the benefit of your heirs.

Net Unrealized Appreciation

One-Time Benefit on Employer Stock Distribution

Many companies maintain retirement plans funded, in whole or in part, with their company's stock. In order to understand the significant benefits that may be available to an investor with company stock held inside a retirement plan, a brief overview of the estate and income tax treatment of retirement plan benefits is helpful. The subsequent paragraphs given in this section will help describe how certain benefits can be achieved when appreciated company stock is held inside a company's retirement plan.

Qualified retirement plans, 401(k) and profit sharing plan, etc. allow employees to defer current earnings (and income tax) until retirement. Furthermore, employers can contribute to such plans on behalf of employees on a pre-tax basis. In order for an employee to access retirement plan funds, he or she must be retired or "separated from service" (i.e., leave the company). Upon retirement or separation, qualified retirement plan benefits can be left in the plan or rolled over tax-free to an Individual Retirement Account (IRA).

When the employee begins distributions from the Plan or the IRA, he or she is taxed on the amount distributed. These distributions are treated as "ordinary income" for tax purposes. If distributions begin after retirement but before a certain age (generally, 55 for retirement plan distributions, assuming retirement on or after age 55, and 59½ for IRA distributions), an "early withdrawal" penalty tax of 10% could be assessed. Additionally, qualified retirement plan benefits are subjected to the "required minimum distribution" ("RMD") rules that require a minimum amount be distributed from the account once you reach age 70½[8]. For estate planning purposes, these assets tend to be less flexible than "non-retirement" assets and are potentially subjected to two layers of tax at death (estate and income), which could substantially reduce the ultimate value of the passed on benefit.

While a retirement plan funded with (appreciated) company stock is subject to the pros and cons of other retirement plans as discussed above, there are certain income and estate tax benefits available. These include the ability to:

- Convert "ordinary income" into tax-advantaged "capital gain" income

- Use employer stock to fund a spouse's estate

- Obtain substantial charitable contribution benefits

- Avoid the RMD rules

There are many complex tax rules that need to be reviewed when contemplating this technique. Under current tax law, special benefits are afforded to appreciated employer stock held inside an employer retirement plan (Section 402(e) (4)). At retirement or separation from service, an employee is eligible to withdraw the employer stock from the retirement plan and treat those shares (going forward) as "non-retirement" assets. This allows you to convert retirement assets into non-retirement assets and you may be able to do this at reduced income levels at the time of distribution, resulting in potentially lower taxes. Under current tax law, the amount of the distribution treated as "ordinary income" (and subject to ordinary income tax rates similar to other retirement plan distributions) is equal to the employer's cost basis on the shares. Tax on the excess value, equal to the market value at the date of distribution less the employer's cost basis (referred to as "net unrealized appreciation" or "NUA"), is deferred until the shares are sold. At the time the stock is sold, the NUA is taxed as a long-term capital gain. This is true even if the shares are sold immediately following distribution from the Plan.

But what if you do not want to take all of the employer stock out of the Plan? You can retain a portion of the shares outside of the company retirement plan and "rollover" the remainder of the shares into an IRA. In order to take advan-

---

[8] Current tax law allows the first distribution required to be paid out upon attaining age 70½ to be deferred until April 1 of the year following the year that the participant reaches age 70½.

tage of the available income tax benefits you must ensure the distribution from the Plan qualifies as a "lump sum" distribution.

In addition to benefiting from lower long-term capital gains rates, employer stock distributed from the Plan can be used to fund a spouse's estate. Quite often, a retirement plan represents the largest asset of a family. Many times the worker's spouse does not have sufficient assets in his or her name to fully utilize their estate/gift tax exemption. While it is not possible to transfer retirement plan assets to a spouse without incurring income taxes during your lifetime, employer stock received from the Plan can be transferred for these purposes. There are some very specific, and technical, tax implications that need to be understood with such a transfer.

For those who are charitably inclined, distributing shares of appreciated employer stock from a Company retirement plan is another technique. As previously discussed, the tax you pay when you withdraw the stock from the plan is based upon the employer's cost basis of the shares. However, if these shares are then contributed to a qualified charity (or to a charitable trust), the value of the income tax deduction is based upon the market value of the stock at the time of contribution. The value of the tax deduction can often exceed the amount of income subject to tax as a result of taking the shares out of the Plan. And, as with other gifts of qualified appreciated stock, long-term capital gain tax is avoided. This technique can result in significant income and estate tax benefits and provide benefits to charitable organizations.

As previously mentioned, retirement plan benefits are required to be paid out when you reach age 70½ whether or not you need the money. This could result in the payment of income taxes on these funds earlier than necessary. In contrast, employer stock distributed from a retirement plan is not subject to these rules. If you do not need these assets to live on, utilizing this technique could allow these assets to continue to grow on a tax-deferred basis beyond age 70½. Plus, any appreciation in the stock that exists at death (which arose after the time of distribution from the plan) can potentially be avoided under the "step up" in basis rules, which is beneficial to your heirs.

There are many valuable benefits to properly utilizing appreciated employer stock held inside a retirement plan. However, there are some instances where a distribution may not be the best course of action. Care needs to be taken to ensure all issues are considered prior to making any distribution. The reader is urged to discuss this matter with their financial or tax advisor to understand it clearly and to obtain the maximum benefit.

PART III

Estate Planning

Estate planning is the process of deciding what you want to happen to your estate and taking the action necessary to insure that these wishes are or will be implemented. The purpose of an estate plan is to insure that what you own will be passed on to loved ones in the manner you wish, without too much of the estate going to pay for death taxes and probate costs.

Since a person can begin to pass on an estate while he or she is still living, thus reducing the tax bite for heirs, estate planning is a lot more than preparing a will, which takes effect only after a person dies. Once you have a clear picture of what your estate is, you may want to ask a qualified estate attorney about possible ways to start distributing assets in your lifetime, using such vehicles as trusts and gifts.

Before an estate can be settled and its assets distributed following your death, it must first be reviewed by the probate court. This process can take as much as six months to a year, so estate planning should include such provisions as emergency cash, insurance that pays directly to survivors, joint bank accounts that carry survivors' names, and other devices that will assure survivors of needed income before they can take possession of your estate.

Most people don't normally think of their belongings as an "estate," nor do they worry much about what will happen to it when they're gone from this world; they just assume that their possessions will simply pass on to their families. However, at your death the federal government imposes an estate tax on all property in excess of $1,000,000 (as of this writing) passing from your estate to your heirs—as much as 50 percent of your hard-earned assets. In addition, estate taxes are due in cash within nine months of death.

Use of Different Will/Trust Designs

Revocable Living Trust (RLT)

An RLT is an arrangement by which you transfer ownership of your assets to another entity, a trust. As a "living trust," the transfer of assets must occur during your lifetime. You (the settler) can set up a trust with your own assets and retain management and control of these assets if you act as your own trustee. You can also designate someone else as your trustee; for instance, in the event you become incapacitated.

An RLT is a means by which an individual transfers legal ownership of funds to a trustee with the intention that the funds will be used by the trustee for the benefit of a designated person. A revocable living trust is one in which the trust's grantor reserves the right to revoke the trust. A revocable living trust is established through a written trust document.

Why Do People Set Up An RLT?

The RLT is an ideal arrangement for many for many reasons. An RLT can be used as a substitute for a Will, in that it provides for the distribution of assets upon the settler's death. The trust assets are distributed directly to the beneficiaries and, unlike a Will; there is no automatic court supervision or probate. One advantage is that the allocation of assets is faster and less costly than through distribution pursuant to a Will.

A living trust may also provide for the marital deduction to avoid taxes when assets are transferred to a surviving spouse, and may minimize taxes against heirs by preserving the uniform tax credit available to the estate of the first spouse to die. Additionally, challenges to a revocable trust are difficult and costly, which may discourage potential Will contests.

Why It Could Be A Mistake?

Under a living trust, there is no ongoing court supervision of the trustee; therefore there is less protection if the assets are mismanaged. A living trust costs more to draft than a Will; these expenses occur during your lifetime, as opposed to probate costs paid by heirs. Transferring ownership of all your assets to the trust can be a lengthy process. Many financial advisors recommend also drafting a Will, to ensure that any assets not captured by the RLT are transferred upon the settler's death. Since a living trust must be fully funded to function effectively, it may require considerable effort by the settler to manage. Also, in many states, an RLT cannot shield your assets should you be facing the prospect of long-term care.

The RLT is one vehicle to consider when drafting an estate plan. But remember, your plan should outline your unique financial objectives and personal values. What works for someone else, even a family member, may not be the best plan for you.

Irrevocable Life Insurance Trust (ILIT)

An Irrevocable Life Insurance Trust is used to hold a life insurance policy outside of an estate in order to avoid income and estate taxes. Because the trust is a separate entity from the insured's estate, the life insurance is not a part of the net worth and therefore not subject to estate tax. Life insurance death benefits are not subject to income tax; therefore, the proper use of an Irrevocable Life Insurance Trust will enable the heirs to receive the death benefit free and clear of estate and income tax.

To minimize taxes and maximize flexibility:

- The ILIT must be irrevocable and "funded" properly.
- If a spouse is a beneficiary, community property cannot be used to fund the trust.
- The settler (trust creator) should not be the trustee or a beneficiary.
- The settler may have the power to remove and replace a trustee but cannot change beneficiaries.
- The trustee cannot be authorized to pay the estate tax.
- For greatest flexibility, an ILIT should be a "grantor trust" for income tax purposes, and it should contain provisions related to non-cash assets.
- An ILIT can be designed as a generation-skipping trust, including a "dynasty trust".

Types of Irrevocable Trusts

Irrevocable Trusts—Generally: There are a number of types of irrevocable trusts that can be used to make gifts to other persons with the assets under the control and management of a trustee.

- Gifts to an irrevocable trust are sometimes motivated by a desire to minimize federal transfer taxes or to shelter assets from the claims of future creditors and other claimants (including spouses in divorce cases and plaintiffs in civil lawsuits).

- To be effective for estate-reduction purposes, the trust must be irrevocable, and the trust's settler should not be a beneficiary of the trust. It is also best if the settler is not a trustee, either.

- In order to qualify for the $10,000 annual exclusion for gift-tax purposes, irrevocable trusts usually contain a provision giving the trust's beneficiaries a temporary right to withdraw annual contributions, at least in part. This withdrawal right is often called a "Crummey power" in reference to a Ninth Circuit Federal Court case involving a family with the "Crummey" surname.

Minors' Trusts: A trust can be established for younger beneficiaries to provide for education and/or other needs of life. Federal tax law has facilitated the creation of trusts for beneficiaries under the age of 21 years, but trusts can be designed to continue until any age or during a beneficiary's entire lifetime.

Bypass and Spendthrift Trusts: A "bypass trust" is a trust that benefits one or more beneficiaries without being considered assets of those beneficiaries for estate and gift tax purposes. Under state law, a bypass trust can be designed to also qualify as a "spendthrift trust", which cannot be attacked by a beneficiary's creditors. In short, this type of trust can reduce the beneficiaries' estate taxes and protect trust assets from creditors' claims at the same time.

Supplemental Needs Trusts: If an intended beneficiary is a recipient of Medicaid, SSI, or other governmental assistance programs, an outright gift or a gift in trust may disqualify the beneficiary from continuing to receive such assistance. Trusts can be designed so that distributions are made only to "supplement" the benefits already being received. So long as distributions made by the trustee are discretionary and not mandatory, the trust assets and trust distributions are not, under most programs, considered disqualifying resources.

Specialized Trusts: Irrevocable trusts can be designed in an infinite number of ways. There are some very special types of irrevocable trusts that have evolved over the years as basic estate planning tools, including irrevocable life insurance trusts (ILITs) and charitable trusts (CRTs and CLTs). Other irrevocable trusts are relatively new, having been developed recently to replace types of trusts that are not longer permitted by law and to maximize the benefits under current transfer-tax laws.

The A/B or Credit Equivalent Trust

An A-B Trust is one version of a living trust that can be used by married couples to utilize the $1,000,000 exemption for each spouse and thereby minimize or eliminate estate taxes. In the usual "A/B" Trust arrangement, the "A" Trust qualifies for the Marital Deduction. This option is included in all Legacy Documents.

"A" Trust: Also known as a "Marital Trust", the marital trust provides management for assets passed to your spouse. The alternative is to leave assets for your spouse outright (no trust). A trust can add a level of comfort that someone is available to manage the assets. If no restrictions are placed on what happens to the assets at the second death, it's called a general power of appointment. If you choose to control what happens at the second death, you need to establish a Qualified Terminable Interest Property trust or "QTIP" trust (a stricter form of marital trust)[9].

"B" Trust: Also known as a "Family Trust" or a credit equivalent trust, the family trust is funded with up to the maximum assets that can pass with no tax due. These assets are taxed at death, but since each person has a unified credit, no tax is actually due. Once these assets have been taxed (with no tax due), they are free to grow to any amount and will never be taxed again for estate purposes.

---

[9] Often used in second marriages where children are involved, a QTIP trust allows the creator of the trust to determine where his or her assets will ultimately go after the second spouse dies.

The Use of Second-To-Die Insurance

Second to Die Life Insurance is used to reduce the overall cost of a Life Policy and/or provide for funds to cover estate taxes when they are due, typically at the death of the second spouse. These policies are also commonly used in conjunction with a Charitable Remainder Trust to replace a gifted asset for your heirs.

It is primarily used to cover the estate taxes that become due when the second spouse passes away. Because two lives are being insured, it's possible to reduce the over all cost of the policy and also provide coverage when one spouse may not be insurable if they attempted to purchase a policy on their own life individually.

The ownership of a second to die life policy is very important. If the policy is not structured, funded or owned properly it could cause the policy death benefit to be included in the estate of the deceased insured; this would increase the overall estate and create a larger estate tax exposure. Because you want to be sure that the policy has no incidence of ownership by the insured, either family members or an irrevocable life insurance trust owns most policies.

The Best-Way to Go About Second to Die Life Insurance Policy

Because the ultimate cost is based on the underwriting results obtained from medical records, interviews and physical examination that need to be done on the insured individuals, the final cost isn't known until the underwriters have reviewed all the material information. An illustration is provided prior to underwriting to give a best efforts estimate based on preliminary information provided to the agent. The best way to proceed with this type of policy purchase is to review an initial illustration and determine if the policy suits your needs and goals. If so, submit an application and go through the underwriting procedure. There is no cost for this and it is the only way to determine your true policy premiums.

Living Wills

With the technological advancements in medicine, people are faced with increasingly difficult ethical decisions concerning medical treatment and care, especially in terminal situations. For some people, the possibility of extended life is meaningful and beneficial. For others, artificial prolongation of life may seem to provide nothing medically necessary or beneficial, serving only to extend suffering and prolong the dying process. Today, people regularly live long past the time they cease to be "functional." You can naturally outlive your capacity to function in a day-to-day sense, such as making decisions regarding your finances. And with tools such as respirators, modern medicine has also made it possible for you to survive even after your body has, for all intents and purposes, stopped functioning. Two concerns arise in relation to terminal care. One is the concern that a patient will be kept alive indefinitely by artificial means. The other is that too little care will be given, and a patient will suffer unnecessarily or die prematurely. Now is the time to plan for what you want to happen should such misfortunes arise—after becoming incapacitated, it might be too late. That's why living wills and durable powers of attorney are important parts of an estate plan.

Definition

A living will, also called a Healthcare Directive or a Directive to Physicians, makes known what medical treatments should be used or withheld if you become irreversibly comatose or terminally ill and can't communicate your wishes. Don't assume your spouse or relatives automatically control your medical treatment if you're unable to do so. On the contrary, the courts have ruled that only *you* can make such decisions. Without a living will, your fate lies in the hands of health-care providers.

But a living will alone doesn't assure that health-care providers will adhere to your wishes even if you can't express them. Though you may try to be comprehensive, a document can't account for all possible health-care scenarios. For instance, treatment options may become available that weren't being used when you drew up your living will.

You need to legally designate someone—called variously a health-care surrogate, health-care power of attorney, or health-care proxy—to oversee your medical treatment if you can't. Working in conjunction with your living will, your health-care surrogate assures that strangers or people who were never made aware of your wishes won't decide your fate.

You also should consider what will happen to your property if you become incapacitated. Without making proper provisions, legal wrangling over finances could add to the burden already placed on loved ones by your ill health.

A simple solution exists: Designate to someone the durable power of attorney, making him or her your attorney-in-fact. Despite the implications of the name, attorneys-in-fact need not be lawyers—a spouse or grown child is the most common choice. Your attorney-in-fact will administer your finances and business with as much or as little power as you designate. They'll take such responsibilities as using your assets to pay your family's everyday expenses, filing and paying your taxes and running your small business.

Laws concerning the designation of durable power of attorney vary from state to state, but the process is usually simple and need only be notarized and signed to become legally binding. Power of attorney takes effect as soon as you become incapacitated and terminates upon your death. And unless you want to unnecessarily involve the courts, it's a must for any estate plan.

Difference Between General Will and Living Will

A living Will is a separate document from a general Will. A living Will designates how you wish to be cared for regarding your medical care and treatment while you are still alive if you for some reason cannot specify those wishes yourself. You can designate, for instance, whether you wish to be kept on life prolonging machines if there is no longer any hope that you will recover from, for instance, an accident or long-term terminal medical condition. A living Will is filled out apart from your general Will, which is responsible for directing your wishes about how you want to have your assets distributed once you pass away.

Requirements of Statute

The advance directive for health care (Living Will) requires writing an executed in accordance with the requirements of the state law. It must be either signed and dated in front of an attorney at law or other person authorized to administer oaths, or in the presence of two subscribing adult witness.

If the two adult witnesses are used, they both must attest that the declarant is of sound mind and not under undue influence. A designated health care representative shall not act as a witness to the execution of the advance directive. Since this is a legal document, it must be executed properly to be valid under the statute.

Powers of Attorney

There could come a time when you are unable to act on your own behalf in a legal matter. In such a case, you may grant someone the "Power of Attorney" to act for you by signing a notarized document with the details of the legal matter and the time period for which the document is in effect.

The subsequent paragraphs in this section give a brief summary of the concept of a "Power of Attorney" and their types. Remember the two most important facts about a Power of Attorney: first, the person granting it (the "Principal") must be competent and second, it is of no further effect upon the death of that person.

Definition

A "Power of Attorney" is a document that allows an individual to appoint a person to manage his or her affairs if he or she is unavailable or unable to do so. The person appointed is referred to as an "Attorney-in-Fact" or "Agent."

General Power of Attorney

A General power of attorney authorizes the Attorney-in-Fact to act on behalf of an individual in several of different situations. A general power of attorney is very broad and provides extensive powers to the person appointed as the Attorney-in-Fact. A general power of attorney is usually used to allow the agent to handle all of the principal's affairs during a period of time when he or she is unable to do so. And a general power of attorney is often included as part of an estate plan to make sure that the principal has covered the possibility that he or she might be incapacitated.

These powers usually include: banking transactions, safety deposit boxes, transactions involving U.S. bonds and securities, buying and selling real estate, settling claims, managing stocks and bonds, making gifts, filing tax returns, matters related to government benefits, making gifts, maintaining and operating business interests, and disclaiming interests (this has to do with estate planning strategies to avoid estate taxes).

Special Power Of Attorney

A Special Power of Attorney authorizes the Attorney-in-Fact to act on someone's behalf in specific situations only, such as a real estate transaction.

Health Care Power Of Attorney

A Health Care Power of Attorney authorizes the Attorney-in-Fact to appoint someone to make health care decisions for the person who may be incapacitated.

Durable Power of Attorney

The concept of a Durable Power of Attorney can be included in the general, special and health care powers of attorney. They can each be made "durable" by adding certain language to the document. This means that the power of attorney will remain in effect (or take effect) if the principal becomes mentally incompetent. If he or she becomes mentally incompetent while a power of attorney document is already in effect, a durability provision will allow the document to stay in effect. One can also sign a durable power of attorney document to prepare for the possibility that he or she may become mentally incompetent due to illness or an accident. In this case, he or she would specify that the power of attorney would not go into effect unless a physician certifies that he or she is mentally incapacitated.

Other Considerations

Other considerations for all parties involved are:

- The attorney in fact can be held liable for intentional misconduct. In other words, deliberately performing an act that is either not permitted by the document or intentionally going beyond the powers allowed to him or her.

- Generally, the document provides for a successor agent. In the event that the person named in the power of attorney is incapacitated, dies, or unable to serve for any reason, a successor assumes the role as agent. This is particularly important if a husband and wife hold powers for one another and both are elderly. In that case, a younger person should be named as successor.

- The document must be notarized to ensure that there is no issue as to its validity. In addition, it allows the document to be recorded if it being used to affect the transfer of real estate on behalf of the individual granting the power of attorney.

- Finally, a power of attorney is different from a guardianship. A guardianship requires court approval. While many of the powers are the same, the requirements for obtaining each are very different.

- The person making it can revoke a Power of Attorney.

Titling of Assets—Beneficiaries

How Proper Titling Can Save Your Beneficiaries a Bundle

Titling of assets is of utmost importance, because the way you title your assets can have a major effect on your beneficiaries' inheritance. Titling of assets can serve a variety of purposes. Titling assets strategically can help speed the process of transferring assets to your heirs, can keep your wishes and finances private and can help ensure that your wishes are followed. In addition to how your assets are titled, it is important to consider naming beneficiaries for those assets that you have titled in your name.

What Is Titling Of Assets And How It Can Save In Different Situations?

There are a variety of ways to title assets. You can own property jointly with another person or you can own property individually. When you own property jointly, you can title the assets so they automatically go to your co-owner upon your death, or you can each own individual stakes in the property.

Joint Tenants with Rights of Survivorship (JTWROS) entitles your co-owner to all of the assets in the event of your death.

As Tenants by Entirety (ATBE) is only recognized in certain states and is only applicable for married couples. Titling assets ATBE ensures that your surviving spouse retains all assets in the account and might provide certain protections in the case of a liability lawsuit.

Tenants in Common (TIC) allow each co-owner to retain his or her stake in the account. The ownership then passes to the estate of each owner upon death.

You can also own property as an individual. Some accounts allow you to name beneficiaries, rather than having the assets in those accounts go directly to your estate.

One way to retain individual ownership of property while avoiding probate on accounts that do not allow you to name a beneficiary is to title the property Transfer on Death (TOD).

Transfer on Death (TOD) allows you to retain complete control of the assets during your lifetime while naming a beneficiary upon your death. This form of asset titling is not recognized by all states. TOD accounts remain free from your beneficiary's creditors, and you can change your beneficiary at any time.

Naming beneficiaries: Certain property, such as retirement accounts or life insurance policies allow you to name a beneficiary. If you fail to name a beneficiary for one of your accounts that you own individually, the assets will become part of your estate upon your death. The problem with this version of an estate plan is that all of the assets will go through probate.

Check Your Beneficiary Designations NOW!

You've worked hard to provide for your family's financial security. Unless you take the time to plan now, you may be putting their long-term financial welfare in jeopardy. Providing for them after you are gone takes careful thought, and your first consideration should be whom you want to receive your assets. Getting your financial and legal affairs in order can seem like a daunting task. But if you break it down into small steps, the process actually would become comparatively simple and straightforward. You should eliminate uncertainty and error by taking steps to transfer your assets to the people you want to receive them at your death-by way of assigning beneficiary designations.

Make a complete, up-to-date inventory of your assets—including real estate, investments, bank accounts, insurance policies, annuities and retirement plans. The inventory should identify each asset, the current value of each asset, and the name or names on the title. Also include information about where each asset is held. For assets that pass by beneficiary designation, (life insurance policies, annuities, retirement plans, pay-on-death accounts) list the primary and secondary beneficiaries clearly.

The inventory you prepare will provide a roadmap of your assets for your own use; it also provides a roadmap of your assets for your family to use if you become disabled and at your death. It will also identify any assets that are titled incorrectly. For example, if your spouse owned the house before your marriage, was your name added to the deed? If the inventory reveals that any asset is titled incorrectly, take the necessary steps to correct the title appropriately.

Transfer Methods

At death, assets are transferred by one of four methods:

- **Beneficiary Designation:** for assets that pass by beneficiary designation like life insurance, annuities, IRAs, and some types of bank and investment accounts, make sure that you have named a primary and a secondary beneficiary. Assets that transfer by beneficiary designation pass directly to the beneficiary and avoid probate.

- **Joint Ownership:** assets that pass by joint ownership with rights of survivorship also avoid probate. However, there are risks involved in adding other people's names to the title of your assets. Consult a qualified estate attorney about the risks and the benefits before using joint ownership to transfer your assets.

- **Will:** Assets that pass by will are transferred to the intended recipients through probate court. Most people believe that if they have a will they have avoided probate. It's just the opposite; probate is required for assets passing by will. Probate is also required, in some circumstances, if you die without a will.

- **Living Trust:** Assets that pass by a living trust are transferred to the intended beneficiaries without probate. A trust also allows for great flexibility in the distribution of trust assets. For example, distributions to the beneficiaries can be made in installments over short or long periods of time. This is especially attractive for parents whose children are too young or too immature to manage money.

Beneficiary Designation Checklist

- ✓ Check the default provisions of the document that governs your retirement account, as it may come into effect if your beneficiary predeceases you and you fail to make subsequent changes.

- ✓ Look into the tax implications for the kind of beneficiary you choose, whether a particular person, such as a spouse or non-spouse, an entity, such as a charity, your estate, or a type of trust.

- ✓ Request a confirmation of receipt of the designation from your retirement account trustee, custodian, or administrator. Documents do not always reach their intended recipient and/or may get lost in transit. Beneficiary designations are considered in effect, only if they are received by the responsible party (e.g. trustee, custodian, or administrator) before the retirement account owner dies.

✓ If you prefer to use a customized beneficiary designation, make sure your trustee, custodian, or administrator finds it acceptable. Not all financial institutions or qualified plans will accept customized beneficiary designations.

✓ Check with your financial institution periodically to determine who your beneficiary is—you may need to make changes if you had a change in your family such as a birth, death, divorce, or marriage.

✓ Consult with your financial advisor to determine if your current beneficiary designation is the one best suited for you and/or if you need to make changes.

Making a proper beneficiary designation is very important part of your financial planning. You can carry out many of these steps (but not all the steps), without an attorney. In fact, you will save time if you prepare the inventory, check beneficiary designations and check titles to assets before consulting an attorney. But you should, however, retain an attorney who specializes in estate planning to prepare wills, trusts, powers of attorney and deeds. Be sure to seek competent and expert professional advice regarding assignment of your beneficiary designations.

PART IV

Why I Need a Financial Advisor

The Complexities of a Financial Plan

As financial markets become more complex and difficult to navigate, making financial decisions can seem daunting. With more than 10,000 mutual funds, dozens of retirement plans, separately managed accounts, and other investment options, you have more choices than ever before. Your challenge is to cut through the clutter to choose what's best for you.

Personalized Attention

Financial advisors take time to get to know who you are. The most important information they receive is directly from their clients. Understanding your long-term investment goals and plans enables your financial advisor to assist you in creating a strategy that fits both your objectives and budget requirements.

A Resource for Information

Your financial advisor is your personal financial instructor. From explaining financial terms to providing illustrations on potential investment growth, a financial advisor's goal is to assist you in making educated decisions in regards to your investment portfolio.

Recommendations and Assistance

A financial advisor has the expertise, resources and time to keep abreast of stock market news, legislation and industry trends. A financial advisor can analyze how these trends could affect your investment portfolio. They can provide you with current information and explain how these changes affect your investment styles and objectives.

Ultimately, each investor must make his or her own final decisions, balancing the often-conflicting advice of some of the experts. There are many investment options to choose from and you should feel comfortable with the decisions you make. Investors who choose to invest on their own might find they lack the time, knowledge, and expertise to make informed decisions. In fact, these investors may actually jeopardize their ability to meet long-term objectives.

Going it alone could mean that:

- You rely on tidbits of third-party information (and sometimes misinformation) to make important financial decisions.

- You lose out on valuable opportunities as market conditions change.

- You waste time and energy tracking down answers to your specific questions.

- You end up chasing last year's winners, causing you to buy high or sell low.

- You feel uneasy about volatility, move out of your equity investments, and miss out on market upswings.

No matter what your goals, time horizon, or tolerance for risk, your financial advisor has the professional expertise and insight necessary to help you map out an investment strategy to meet your financial objectives. As your needs change over time, your advisor will be with you every step of the way, monitoring your investments and guiding you through new opportunities. And in times of volatility and uncertainty in the market, you'll get the support you need to maintain your long-term perspective and keep your investment plan on the right track.

Conclusion

My many years in this business have taught me that the one constant in the American economy is change. The stock market will go up, down and sideways; the same can be said of taxes. Although inflation has not presented much of nuisance in recent years, one never knows what the future holds. I've always counseled my clients to keep their portfolios "bulletproof," that is, to protect them from whatever the economy may bring. By employing strategies I've outlined here dear reader and investor, you can do just that. Use correct retirement planning to shelter your nest egg from taxes, make use of estate planning to shelter your legacy from estate taxes and to insure that your assets are distributed according to your wishes, and exercise asset allocation and diversification to protect your portfolio from the volatility of the markets.

I hope you've enjoyed reading this brief guide as much as I've enjoyed writing it! As I said in my preface, I love helping people. Please use "Rolling Over" as a resource to guide you on the road to successful investing. And remember; always seek the guidance of a qualified financial advisor.

Other Useful Resources

There are many resources available on financial planning and estate planning. Here are some that you may find helpful:

- **The Ernst and Young's Retirement Planning Guide**, Bob Garner. Wiley, John & Sons, Inc. 1997. Chapters include 401(k) plans, social security, taxes, insurance, spending and investing in retirement.

- **Set for Life: Financial Peace for People over 50**, Bambi Holzer with Elaine Floyd. Wiley, John & Sons, Inc. 1999. Covers how to assess your needs, manage investments, handle taxes and insurance, stay ahead of inflation, prepare your estate and develop realistic financial goals.

- **IRAs, 401(k)s and Other Retirement Plans: Taking Your Money Out**, Twila Slesnick and John C. Suttle. Nolo Press, 1999. Discusses distribution, penalties and tax options for various retirement plans including traditional and Roth IRAs.

- **Estate Planning Made Easy: Your Step-by Step Guide to Protecting Your Family, Safeguarding Your Assets and Minimizing the Tax Bite**, sec. ed., David T. Phillips and Bill S. Wolfkiel. Dearborn Financial Publishing, Inc., 1998. Includes chapters on ownership and title, wills, trusts and probate.

- **Your Living Trust and Estate Plan: How to Maximize your Family's Assets and Protect your Loved Ones**, Harvey J. Platt. Allworth Press, 1999. A guide to using a living trust to create an estate plan, including discussion of the tax laws.

- **WealthWhen Retirement Planner**, November 1, 2003. WealthWhen Retirement Planner is a new consumer product for exploring a 40 year financial horizon. This product incorporates all the core retirement-planning features of WealthWhen Professional, including intelligent investment portfolio modeling and full federal tax calculations, with a slimmed-down user interface. It is sold with a personal use license, shipped CD, documentation, and 6 months support, and retails at $114.99. Business Week selected WealthWhen in its top three 2003 retirement planning software products. For more details, contact: support@wealthwhen.com

Related Works

- Bernstein, Peter L. (1993). Capital Ideas is a wonderful history of portfolio theory and related topics in finance.

- Bodie, Zvi, Alex Kane and Alan J. Marcus (2002). An investment is the definitive introduction to portfolio theory and related topics in finance.

- Fabozzi, Frank J. and Harry M. Markowitz (2002). Theory and Practice of Investment Management is an essential introduction and reference.

- Grinold, Richard C. and Ronald N. Kahn (1999). Active Portfolio Management is the bible for equity portfolio managers.

- Markowitz, Harry M. (1959). Portfolio Selection is Harry Markowitz's original full-length book on portfolio theory.

- Markowitz, Harry M. (1952). Portfolio Selection, Journal of Finance, 7 (1), 77-91.

- Markowitz, Harry M. (1999). The early history of portfolio theory: 1600-1960, Financial Analysts Journal, 55 (4), 5-16.

About the Author

Jerald L. Aloof, RFC
Managing Director—JL Aloof Financial Services
Registered Financial Consultant

Jerald Aloof has been a practicing financial advisor since 1986 when he began his career in New York City's financial district with EF Hutton & Co.

In 1989, Jerry moved to Dean Witter Reynolds, Inc. in MetroPark, NJ to establish client relationships closer to his home in Central New Jersey. It was at Dean Witter that Jerry met and teamed-up with his partner, David Mattos. David and Jerry moved to PaineWebber, Inc. in November of 1993 where they built their practice together for ten years.

With the industry trend pointing toward independent financial advice, Jerry and David affiliated with Royal Alliance Associates, Inc., a member of the AIG Advisor Group, and formed Mattos Capital Management and JL Aloof Financial Services in May, 2003. This move has allowed them to provide their clients with superior independent financial advice.

Jerry and David are unique in the servicing of their clients. Along with their dedicated service staff, Jerry and David regularly communicate with, and meet face-to-face with almost all of their clients on a quarterly basis.

Jerry and David specialize in Retirement Planning, particularly in the area of Retirement Plan Rollovers. They pride themselves on their integrity, and it's that integrity that instills confidence in their clients. Their grasp of the capital markets combined with their ability to tailor investment programs has helped David and Jerry earn their clients' loyalty. The high degree of their clients' satisfaction is evidenced by the fact that many of David and Jerry's clients refer their friends and relatives to also take advantage of their services.

Jerry Aloof lives in Edison, New Jersey with his wife, Rachelle. They have six children, Shaynde, Daniella, Dov, Goldie, Moshe and Elleonna.

0-595-33544-6

www.ingramcontent.com/pod-product-compliance
Lightning Source LLC
Chambersburg PA
CBHW030911180526
45163CB00004B/1792